MARKETING
medicine

Healthy advice on the
practise of Marketing

Chris Harrison

© 2019 by Christopher James Harrison

Revised first edition: August 2019

All rights reserved. No part of this publication may be reproduced, distributed, or transmitted in any form or by any means, including photocopying, recording, or other electronic or mechanical methods, without the prior written permission of the publisher, except in the case of brief quotations embodied in critical reviews and certain other non-commercial uses permitted by copyright law. For permission requests, write to the publisher, addressed "Attention: Permissions Coordinator," at the address below.

PO Box 15756 – 00509 Nairobi, Kenya

ISBN: 978-1-09-693395-3

Cover design: Ali Bush, Nairobi, Kenya
ali.bush@thebrandinside.com

Typesetting: David Siddall Multimedia, Monmouth, UK
www.davidsiddall.com

Dedication

Dedicated to the four people who made this anthology possible:

Alice Blanchard – who said 'writing is the best therapy'.

Suzanne and Brett Sievwright – who bought me the time.

Atty Harrison – whose confidence never wavered.

Sincere thanks also go to Mike Dickson for his editorial pencil, Ali Bush for her inspiring cover design and Daniel Kariuki for his stylish photography.

Asanteni sana.

CONTENTS

Foreword vii

Chapter 1
Brand Management 1
Chapter 2
Setting Strategy 23
Chapter 3
Seeking Insights 47
Chapter 4
Target Identification 69
Chapter 5
Choosing Channels 93
Chapter 6
Getting Creative 113
Chapter 7
Public Profile 133
Chapter 8
Brand Delivery 151

About the author 171

Foreword

This is a book about Marketing, that just happens to originate in Africa. Marketing is a global practice, and Africa is one of the seven Continents on which it thrives. Make that six – unless you know of any brands being built in Antarctica.

Africa is unusual in still being a place where a keen interest in humanity is encouraged. Where people take an active interest in one another's health and happiness. That's important for Marketers because their discipline is all about understanding human behaviour. You can't change an established consumer habit, or promote a new one, unless you understand its origins. So, expert Marketers develop a working understanding of social anthropology, behavioural psychology and any other 'ology that provides useable insights on the human condition.

Africa is a Continent filled with consumers. Most of them young, and all of them growing savvier by the second thanks to the near-ubiquity of the Internet. Changes in consumer behaviour; growth and decline of market categories; broadening horizons of business opportunity and profound social change are all happening here at an unprecedented pace.

Africa has been my home and my business focus for twenty-five years. It has furnished me with ample opportunity for success and failure. As I have worked to build and deliver brands, whole economies have transformed around me. Not always for the better, but usually in ways that could be described as 'progress'.

For the past decade, I have given myself the task of observing the impact of Marketing on the economies of East Africa. Thanks to the indulgence of the Fourth Estate, this content has appeared every week in newspaper columns and online pages in Africa and across the wider world. At one point, thanks to William Pike of The Star newspaper in Kenya, we branded it Marketing Medicine: the idea being to serve a weekly tonic to jaded business palates.

This eponymous book takes a selection of those observations and groups them into chapters that hope to make sense of the key aspects of Marketing. This is categorically not a textbook – more of a clarifier and a catalyst. For those interested in business anthropology it also charts a dozen years of rapid commercial development in East Africa. If anything I wrote during that time now appears prescient, no one will be more delighted than I.

I commend this book to senior executives who employ Marketers, to inform their expectations. To young people who aspire to be Marketers, to balance their academic learning. And also to the present generation of Marketers, in the expectation that it will give them food for thought. Dum spiro, spero.

Nairobi, Kenya
January 2019

Chapter 1

Brand Management

Building a brand is the most valuable output of Marketing. A brand is many things, but one thing it is not is just a logo. The logo, or graphic and typographic mark, simply exists to signal the presence of the brand. To do so it should be as clear and distinctive as possible.

Branding first began as a burnt mark on the hide of a domesticated animal. Used as a mark of ownership, it came to be a mark of value for those happy herders who raised healthy livestock. I always tell my clients that if they have a logo you can burn onto the rump of a cow and read at ten metres distance, you have a logo that works!

But the logo is valueless if it is meaningless. If a consumer sees a logo, but has no idea what that signifies. So, when Marketers build a brand, they are actually building a value proposition. Our brand is what we do and how we do it. It combines functional delivery – for example a moisturising soap – with emotional benefit: 'Women feel more beautiful'.

Strong brands quite literally add value to businesses. As I write, the most valuable brand in the world is Apple, some way ahead of second place Google. To buy that brand you would need to pay the owner US$182.8 Billion (according to Forbes). Just for the brand – not for the software, the people, the intellectual property or the physical assets of the company.

Strong brands matter to customers because they make buying choices easier. Brands reassure customers that they have made the right choice. And they give we, the consumers, the confidence to try new offerings from the same source. In East Africa, the launch of mobile money solution MPESA would never have been so swiftly successful had the brand provenance not been Safaricom.

In this, our first chapter, we explore the basics of Brand Management.

Proof that brand building works

Let's start out with an African branding success story. It's nice to highlight a brand from East Africa – especially as it proves that Marketing can actually deliver the desired revenue.

Recently I met with a group of investors who have created a successful new brand in eleven months. The reason for the meeting was to plan a session with new investors who were interested in taking the brand to the next level. Note I used the word brand, because it was brand rather than company that attracted their interest. Brands do that.

The initial group of investors came together to create a profitable social enterprise with a clear business purpose: 'To utilise local forestry resources to raise a rural community out of poverty, whilst educating the urban middle class on the importance of conserving the Environment.'

They very carefully and explicitly defined their primary target audience – an urban dweller whose eyes needed to be opened to Nature. They called him (or her) Kim. They pictured Kim as about 37 years old, married with two kids. Currently a Sales Manager at an international tyre distribution company, but with a career spanning several different jobs i.e. Bank Teller, Pharmaceutical Sales Representative, Customer Service Executive. Kim's week is all about work and work-related socialising. At weekends, he/she prefers to share time with spouse and kids – but is often too tired to do much more than visit shopping malls or chill on the couch at home with a movie. Kim's family occasionally dabbles in local tourism, but few safari lodges offer a range of activities the whole family would leave the couch for.

So the initial investors created a product that would deliver shared excitement for Kim's whole family. An outdoor adventure experience in a beautiful forested environment offering zip lining, mountain biking, fly fishing, camping, archery, paintballing and horse riding. With plans and space for an increasing range of activities, and increasing educational opportunities.

The team shaped a clear brand promise and personality, from which they were able to brief and select an absolutely appropriate name – The Forest. They swiftly followed this up with an impactful brand logo and a website **www.theforest.co.ke**. As a result of this focus, they found that they needed to invest surprisingly little money in promoting their brand – social media recommendations and (free) broadcast media features drove enquiries.

On the brand delivery side, they harnessed youthful enthusiasm and a fair chunk of investment from the rural community surrounding their site. Indeed 84% of the workforce come from villages in the immediate vicinity and they have been trained in a range of hospitality, catering, activity management and ancillary skills. 800 members of that community came together to invest an amazing total of US$200,000 cash in the venture, and are actively represented at Board level. (This 'hands in pockets' investment is virtually unknown in community engagement in Africa.)

It's little surprise, then, that their clearly defined performance targets have been smashed. Aiming for 40,000 visitors in 24 months, they have achieved 34,000 in 11 months and numbers continue to climb. Family visits at weekends have been bolstered by corporates looking for the space and facilities to conduct effective team-building sessions.

And no surprise that the second wave of investors have now willingly joined the first, to back the construction of an eco-lodge on the site. And as I write, potential Rwandese investors are asking for a replica site to be created outside Kigali.

Perhaps the only irony of the story is that not one member of the initial team would claim to be a professional Marketer. So, the great thing about Marketing is this: you don't have to hold a vocational qualification to do it well. And many of the common-sense principles that these investors applied will now be explained and illustrated in the chapters that follow.

First published December 2017

The making of a Brand Manager

Let's go right back to the beginning of Brand Management. It started with a memo penned by a young graduate employee of Procter & Gamble, on 13th May 1931.

Neil McElroy was then responsible for the promotion of Camay Soap, and he became frustrated about having to compete not only with external brands but also with internal competitors like P&G's flagship brand – Ivory.

In a memo that broke established P&G rules (running to three pages, when single page communication was mandatory) he outlined the case for a specific team to work on each major brand in their portfolio.

This team was to devote itself to thinking about the Marketing of that brand, and should treat itself as much as possible as a standalone business. In this way, argued McElroy, the qualities of each brand would be distinguished from every other. The target audiences would be clearly delineated to avoid brands knocking spots off each other within the Company's own portfolio.

This made so much sense to P&G's President Deupree that he moderated the punishment for the lengthy memo (perhaps consigning McElroy to a mere six hours in the stationery cupboard) and made the proposal into law.

P&G being who they were (and still are), it will not surprise you to know that their first requirement for a successful Brand Manager was the ability to gather intelligence and analyse it.

If Salesmen were the infantry in the battle to win consumer attention, said McElroy, then Marketers should first and foremost be the intelligence officers. Brand Managers should be able to understand their product within its competitive environment. To fit the pieces of the business puzzle together. To identify the insights that would lead to commercial breakthroughs. It won't surprise you to learn that Neil McElroy later went on to be Secretary for Defense under President Eisenhower in the opening years of the Cold War. So, his insistence on keen intelligence and sharp analysis later had world-defining effects.

Today, any CEO should expect a Brand Manager he employs to produce clear opinion on the commercial opportunities facing the brand. In which market segment it should compete. Against which other brands, and how. At which price point and with how much promotional investment. This opinion should be underpinned by the clearest possible analysis of sales figures and competitor investment levels, identifying trends to be countered or exploited.

A CEO should also expect his Brand Manager to know the target audience for her brand as if they were members of her own family. None of this nonsense about, 'peri-urban women aged 25–35, in the C1C2 socio-demographic group.' Brand Managers should use the language of humanity to paint the richest possible picture of the prospective buyer. 'Our target is a working mum in her mid-Thirties, with too many responsibilities and not enough time to do things as well as she would like ...'

So, a Brand Manager must be able to interpret Market Research and use it as a tool to build complete consumer understanding. If knowledge really is power, then the Marketer who doesn't understand her target audience is truly ineffectual.

Most importantly, a CEO should require a Brand Manager to create rational arguments for investment behind her brand. And demonstrate personal responsibility for the predicted return on that investment.

Sales people usually have a simple relationship with Brand Managers. It tends to be based on contempt and fueled by an envy that is not always justified. But Brand Managers don't help themselves.. They work at a desk – not on the road – and their career is widely perceived to be more fashionable than serious. They are famous for demanding sales information, but rarely give analysis and feedback in return. But sales people are also fallible. They place huge emphasis on what the Trade says, without filtering it. And they deal in tactics, not strategy.

Wikipedia says:

'Brand Management as a business technique was one of the signal innovations in American Marketing during the Twentieth Century. It epitomised the persistent theme of balancing centralised oversight with decentralised decision-making, based on who in the company had the best information about the decision at hand.'

But now, I trust, you have a clearer understanding of Brand Management than Wikipedia does.

First published October 2010

A career in Brand Management

The ability to create and grow brand equity is a crucial skill in any economy. Without brands, an economy only grows in the flat dimension of volume, not in the multiple dimensions of value.

Brands build national wealth, and often help to define the national brand itself. What would Germany be without Mercedes, Audi, Deutsche Bank or Lufthansa? What would Japan be without Sony and Toyota, or South Korea without LG and Hyundai?

Without living brands to care for, too many large enterprises become arrogant and begin to atrophy. Not perhaps in the first decade, but certainly in the second and third. The share price becomes the defining standard. Commercial bureaucracies grow up: built on Finance and Procurement; on benchmarking and just-in-time; on HR and ISO. But all these activities are inward-looking, and add no lasting value.

In this context, it should worry us that the skills, qualifications and experiences which produce people capable of branding are not greatly valued in Africa. When it comes to developing Marketers, we appear to be stuck in a Developing Market rut. We begin poor and uneducated; as we grow we place value on education and we focus on traditional career paths. The Doctor, the Accountant and the Lawyer. This is a reflection of our overwhelming desire for security, for being part of the status quo.

Is it any wonder that our brightest and best go abroad for education and then stay there? They choose to apply their entrepreneurial and creative skills in markets where these things are lauded. For at home they would be regarded as 'not serious'.

People who can brand are by their very nature both creative and entrepreneurial. They look at a market and see a consumer opportunity. Then they disrupt best practises because these are based on what has been, not what can be. The good news is that many of these people exist in Africa.

I recently spent 4 days in the Namib desert with thirty bright young people. Were we on a junket? No, there were no shops or bars around. Were we teambuilding? No, because teambuilding is a decade-old concept whose value is largely spent. Were we writing our mission statement? No, because we had a mission statement which was written in 1923. It contained three words, 'Resist The Usual', which ring as true today as they did then.

All we had to do was to redefine execution. We were there to consider how to change mass behaviour in Africa in the next 12 months. We were reviewing our brand-building achievements of the past year, but then filing them away because we knew the year in prospect had to be different. We were clearing our desks and getting ready to disrupt again.

We could not have done this with people who were conformists, or good administrators or reliable producers. Some of these young people came from artistic backgrounds; some were trained as Lawyers or Journalists; some were Marketers. All had migrated to the Advertising Agency environment. A place that encourages you to ask 'what if?' rather than decide 'why not'. I strongly feel that we need to gather more people like these. Their energy and ideas make the impossible seem achievable. So, let me frame a career choice for young people who want to resist the usual.

Imagine a career where you can work in several industries every day: sausages in the morning; an airline for lunch; and petroleum in the afternoon. Imagine a career where your boss cares more about what the consuming public thinks than the shareholders. Imagine a job where merit can take you from the mailroom to the boardroom.

If this appeals, then you should consider a career in branding. If you are good at ideation you should explore the Agency world – Advertising, Direct Marketing, PR, Experiential. If you are more analytical and deliberate, your first step should probably be Brand Management. Over the next few chapters, we'll touch on what makes a great Agency person, and what a capable Brand Manager does for his Company. There are some myths to dispel, and some practices to challenge.

First published March 2010

Brand Management demands strong relationships

I can't think of one single Brand Manager who has succeeded without the support of others. No matter how self-confident, well-dressed or smartly educated. So, I am of the view that the successful Brand Manager uses human relationships as a 'force multiplier' in developing and executing great Marketing programmes.

Let us consider the internal structure of any Company that employs a Brand Manager. Beginning at the very top, the Brand Manager must be able to maintain a dialogue 'beyond her years' with the CEO and his Executive Board. Challenging though this may seem, the young person should be able to talk in plain language to the most senior people in the Company.

These people are the only ones who have a real overview of the business, and will decide whether or not to support the actions recommended by the Brand Manager. I like to think of it as an episode of 'Dragon's Den', where callow youth meets hoary critique.

Marketing contributions are not best judged by cold rational or financial analysis. Indeed, the Brand Manager should be made to feel the passion that drove her seniors to create the business.

Some Brand Managers will excel in this environment. They will rise to the debate. The challenges posed will force them to sharpen their logic, and their planning will be better for it.

Others, by dint of an educational system that places too much emphasis on rote learning, will fail. They will retreat into obfuscation, and fall back on jargon. They'll come out with terms like Leverage, Search and Spin, Brand DNA, and Salience. The latter is actually a rather good word, but research shows that only 1 in 5 million Marketers knows what it means.

I never equate big words with big ideas. In my experience, the opposite is often the case. So, CEOs and Executive Board members must not let the bluffers through.

Below the C Suite, good Brand Managers build working relationships with Heads of Department inside in the Company. The operational leaders of Production, Sales, Distribution, Customer Experience and Finance. Successful Brand Managers make the effort to walk around inside the Company and understand the value these different disciplines contribute. While they are there, they can also ask what help a Department needs. Demonstrating an interest, and returning with good ideas and solutions, is the way a Brand Manager markets himself and builds his own brand equity.

Broad relationships inside and across the Company give the Brand Manager valuable business insights with which to improve his plans. They also create a base of supporters who can lend a hand when a real problem occurs. Which it undoubtedly will.

First published September 2011

The brand leadership reality check

Nearly every Brand Manager I talk to wants theirs to be the brand leader. But let's have a reality check: brand leadership is easy to say, but very hard to achieve. And it is not always what the business needs.

Many wild hopes are written into Brand Plans, and many bold promises are made to company boards. But the reality on the supermarket shelves, and in the hearts and minds of consumers, can be harsh.

Small brands have it easy, provided they keep their ambitions in check. If you are the No.3 skin lotion, you know where to get your volume from: you go after the big brands. If you invest in competitor activity data you can see what they are doing and outflank them. You try different tactics – price point, emotional connection, trade relations, regional focus. You have little to lose, and much to gain.

Or you can strive to become a niche brand. But, if you do, you must stay tremendously focused. Niche brands deliver something very relevant to a very tightly defined audience. They choose a certain sort of person, and use their loyalty to build word of mouth among more of the same people. Very rarely do they broaden their appeal.

But most Marketers aspire to work on leading brands, which is a much harder job. With a big brand, it's devilishly difficult to squeeze another 10 share points out of the category. Everyone has heard of it, so brand awareness gains achieve very little. Most of the target audience have already tried it, so you may face the dismal task of asking them to rethink why they don't use it.

And if you then decide to regain their commitment, you must adjust what they don't like about the brand. Marketers call this repositioning. Sometimes this works. But often you lose what the brand originally stood for, and then you fail. And while you focus on defending your category leadership position, you may lose sight of lateral threats. Pepsi and Coke have spent decades bashing each other in the fight for sugary drink supremacy. But, while they were fighting, water, juice, tea and coffee brands woke up. Water became Evian, Perrier, Highland Spring, Keringet and Rwenzori. Coffee became Starbucks, News Café, Dormans, Star Café and Java. British Airways was Europe's leading airline until it came up against a music retailer called Virgin and a car hire company called Easy.

So, if you aspire to manage a big brand, my advice is to think hard about what you want to do with it. You will benefit from good consumer research, but research alone will neither solve a problem nor seize an opportunity. What you will really need is the courage and authority to make a big call. To set a clear direction and pursue it long after everyone else in the Company has become bored with it.

If I had my time again, I'd manage a challenger brand. A number 2, 3 or 4. That's where the opportunity lies; where true entrepreneurship and the power of ideas can make you money and make you famous.

Do you still want to manage a brand leader? Of course, you do. Just be careful to choose the right one.

First published January 2012

Here are 5 tips to help you manage brands more successfully

▶ Branding Tip 1 – always tell the truth

Every American knows the charming tale of the young George Washington and the cherry tree. First told by Reverend Mason L Weems in 1800, it symbolised the simple moral character of that new nation's citizens. It did Parson Weems no harm either, as his book ran to more than 40 editions.

Young George had tried his little axe on the bark of his father's prized cherry. Barking the tree condemned it to a slow death, and George's irate father wanted to know who had committed this heinous act. After a moment's deliberation, America's future first President is said to have replied:

'I cannot tell a lie Father; you know I cannot tell a lie! I did cut it with my little hatchet.''

The proud Washington parent forgave his son with these words:

'My son, that you should not be afraid to tell the truth is worth more to me than a thousand trees!'

And it is honesty, and not over-claim or falsehood, that should be the mark of a professional Marketer. For over a century the best Marketers have been in the business of communicating product benefits in a clear and authoritative way. They have broadcast messages to a sometimes interested, but oft-times indifferent, general public. And because of the limitations of conventional media, they have rarely been troubled by consumers answering back.

Many distilleries or cosmetics companies have had no need to converse with consumers unless their teeth have fallen out or their skin turned silver. But there must have been countless times when consumers wanted a little clarification to help them with their purchase decisions. Imagine a cake stall, run by Mr. Joe.

'Buy my cakes!' yells Mr. Joe at passing shoppers. 'They are all very tasty, each with a unique lemony zing!'

'I don't like the look of them,' says Mama Sarah, passing with her basket, 'in fact, each one looks a bit different.'

'They're not very lemony either,' adds Mama Jane, 'And I believe they will be full of preservatives.'

Luckily, Mr. Joe's wife decides to take over the conversation:

'Of course, each one is different,' she says,' They are all home-made by me, not by a machine in a factory. And they don't taste very lemony, because that takes citric acid to artificially boost the zing. And if I didn't use preservatives, they would go mouldy by the weekend. Are you sure that's what you want?'

Mr. Joe is Marketing in a traditional way, and not used to being questioned. But Mrs. Joe is more prepared to address real customer feedback. From the consumers' viewpoint, Mrs. Joe seems to be telling the truth whereas Mr. Joe may be a liar.

Every day in Africa, the reach of the Internet expands. In this new space, Marketers are coming face-to-face with consumer opinion for the first time. Consumers now give immediate reviews and opinions. Other consumers read them and comment. These opinions can't be bought off, or threatened with advertising blackouts. That used to work with newspaper editors, but it won't work with Mama Sarah. What to do?

Well, the interesting thing is that brands that are more honest with consumers tend to win greater loyalty. This is not new. In the 1930's GM ran powerful advertisements intending to persuade people to buy one of their cars over a Ford or a Packard. But first it asked them to 'try all three.' Volkswagen admitted the Beetle was ugly. Avis Car Rental has allowed that they haven't always got it right. When the Virgin Atlantic's in-flight entertainment system fails, the cabin crew apologises to you in person and offers you a gift (air miles). But on some other airlines you don't even get an extra helping of chicken or beef. So, when the consumer answers back, be ready.

Be prepared to admit that your user guide isn't very clear. That ticket machines always require intervention from an attendant. That your beer contains preservatives that may make hangovers worse.

Analyse consumer reviews, and then get your Ad Agency to change its copywriting. Moderate the tone of your advertising from mindless cheerleading to something more human and engaging. Marketers are not great at admitting weakness. We often claim that our radio station 'appeals to everyone', or that our product can 'shine teeth and clean gums'. But instead, how about making it clear to consumers what your brand is not good for?

General Carl Von Clausewitz said that the essence of strategy was sacrifice. As brand builders, let's take care not to sacrifice the truth.

First published June 2010

▶ Branding Tip 2 – get out of the office

You can learn a lot more about your brand and its competitors by getting away from your desk and getting into 'the field'. Here's what happened when I did just that quite recently. In a rural market where a client intended to launch their brand.

It was a long, hot, dusty day ... but a very valuable one. I saw retail premises as smart and as well-displayed as you would find in any capital city. These shops bore little relation to the dark and grubby dukas, kiosks and kafundas of old. Places where the merchandise and staff were separated from the customers by wire mesh. Where torn and defaced product posters overlapped along peeling walls. Where customer service was dead-eyed and dull.

These new shops had tiled floors, glass display cabinets, bright lighting and smart point-of-sale materials displayed in a disciplined way. The sales staff were out in the middle of the shop, talking to customers. The whole impression was very professional. These weren't the kind of places that, at dusk, convert into makeshift bars to garner more revenue. They were in business to make buying a more enjoyable experience for the customer.

We toured a large market town, looking for cues on how best to tackle the rollout. Local intelligence identified an area of schools and universities, a central business and government district, and a sizeable open market. This enabled us to plot different Marketing approaches to different target audiences by location. We did this as a collaborative exercise between the client's Sales and Marketing leaders. It worked very well, and produced a balanced consensus on the parameters of the launch plan.

You may think there is nothing remarkable about this. You would say it makes absolute sense for the two market-facing departments in the business to work together from the outset. To get out on the ground together and gather the insights that create success. But it is remarkable because, in many companies, key departments keep themselves separate. They pursue their own agendas. They perpetuate a stereotypical view of each other's strengths and weaknesses. So, when a very visible project forces them out into the open, their primary focus is on avoiding blame for poor performance.

This is not a failure of capability or capacity; it's a failure of business culture. Sales teams believe that they drive revenues, win against competitors and build the relationships the business depends upon. They expect Marketers to produce the support materials they need, and to join them on the ground when the action hots up. They believe that Marketers are reluctant to leave the comfort of their own offices.

By contrast, Marketers tend to see salespeople as glory-seeking footsloggers, who don't get the big picture. They resent producing materials to a Sales brief, and they try to hold on to the high ground of branding.

As a business leader, a CEO must be able to address such unhelpful behaviours before they damage the performance of the brand. And a good way to do this is to force the protagonists to confront the business realities out there in the market, standing on the ground together.

First published February 2017

▶ Branding Tip 3 – fit for purpose

Travel, they say, broadens the mind. It throws up new ideas and insights. In foreign countries, you encounter new brands. You also have to rely on the brands you carry with you from home. Sometimes they are fit for purpose, sometimes not. And the truth is, if a brand does not do what it promised to do, no amount of Marketing whitewash will save it.

In Milan, Italy, the taxis are a modern wonder. When you call for one, it is done digitally. You get a printout from a terminal, showing the taxi number and the time it will arrive – usually within 3 minutes. It often arrives ahead of time. Usually the vehicle is a

Toyota Prius. Silent and swift, and only using its petrol engine on long, fast roads. In a country of petrolheads, this alternative energy car has been embraced for very practical economic reasons. Milan taxis are fit for purpose, and fast becoming part of that city's brand. In many cities Uber is offering a similar service. That's brand competition for you: markets don't stand still.

In Germany, I confidently used the peer recommendation site **www.tripadvisor.com** to arrange car hire and to book four hotels in different towns. Because consumer ratings drive the site, you arrive with a good idea of what each hotel will be like. You even see photographs posted by departing guests. For some reason, when Germans post, their little albums always begin with a picture of the bathroom, or more specifically the lavatory. Reassuring us that, in this world of change, some things remain constant.

The German airline Lufthansa no longer has check-in desks. You swipe your passport at a terminal, choose your seat, print your boarding pass and dump your bag. Even at peak times this reduces check-in to less than 10 minutes. Other airlines have 'stolen' this idea too, because it works.

Flying home on Kenya Airways, their fabled flatbed (excellent when it works) did not work. In fact, 2 out 20 beds didn't (10% failure on a product that costs USD 4000 for a round trip to Europe). As the long-suffering and very helpful purser wrestled a third bed flat using manual override, I asked her an important question. 'Do you report technical problems?' 'Oh yes', she replied, leaving me to wonder how these very basic defects had neither been rectified nor the cabin crew informed. Kenya Airways flat bed, often unfit for purpose.

I travel with technology. I use my iPhone to navigate, to find ATMs, restaurants and petrol stations. I connect with friends on Foursquare. I check in on Facebook. And I have to fight the email dragon. But I can only do that if my GSM network works. I use three networks at home in Kenya. On a recent trip I had a real opportunity to compare and contrast. I ran my iPad on Safaricom data roaming. It didn't work initially and required an eight hour on-off conversation with a Safaricom customer service person to sort it out. But I stuck with it, and so did she. I was impressed.

My iPhone uses the thrice-renamed network, Bharti Airtel. All over Africa, customers have received declining service levels: first with Celtel, then with Zain, and now with Airtel. Each 'rebranding' involved a million litres of paint, and made billboard contractors rich. In no case was it a true rebranding, because not one African consumer received a clear message about how the change would really benefit them. In the last month, I have turned to Airtel for help to activate data roaming in Uganda (their own network), Paris, Dusseldorf, Cologne, Amsterdam and Milan. They failed comprehensively. In each case their conclusion was 'it's all alright on our end.' But the reality was a network unfit for purpose.

Airtel customer service people were really saying, 'You're on your own, so sod you.' So now it's my turn to play that back. To the GSM network that has so far done more than any other to commoditise and downgrade Africa's mobile experience, I say, 'Airtel you're on your own, so...'

First published October 2011

▶ Branding Tip 4 – make the basics brilliant

If you are successful in business, you tend to drive yourself quite hard. If you are a competent brand owner or manager you often set ambitious goals for your brand. Aim high is what we are told to do. But sometimes it may be worth pausing to consider those goals more objectively. Taking out the emotion; damping the enthusiasm with a touch of realism. If you don't, you may be creating an unnecessarily hard rod for your own back.

The reality is that very few consumers are as interested in your brand as you are. They live out there, in the real world of brand claim and counterclaim. A world of pleasant yet enduring boredom, frequent disappointment and occasional flashes of brilliance.

In real-life conversation, if you say to the ordinary man in the street: "Bank with me, because I am going to be your long-term partner, delivering innovative financial solutions in a caring way" he would rightly consider you demented. Yet I heard exactly this claim, or something very similar, from a pan-African bank last night on television. And even if that bank could deliver on such a utopian ideal, I'm still not sure it is the bank I need.

I spend much of my time in the meeting rooms of the mighty. Privy to the conversations that happen inside the companies that manage the best-known brands in our markets. But, increasingly, I find myself asking them for a reality check. Because the brand offering does not fit the market need. Instead it aspires to exceed an imagined need ... without any good reason.

Instead of aiming too high, I recommend they focus on getting the basics right for their customers. If you are in the broadcast production business, do you really need to produce the highest definition TV content? Beautifully lit. With smooth panning, jump cuts, dissolves and more clever camera work? With models who know how to act and make-up artists who understand about forehead sheen and lighting contrast? Probably not, judging by the technical quality of TV signal still received by most African audiences.

If you are in the petroleum business, must you really challenge yourselves to distribute high performance fuels that might, in other markets and in more modern vehicles, squeeze an additional mile per gallon, or extra hour of life from a motor engine? Probably not, if your vehicle population has an average age of 12 years and is maintained by informal roadside mechanics.

So why bother setting expectations if you know you may not meet them? Instead, tell your customers that you understand what they need, and settle on providing that. This, of course, assumes that you have accurately identified what they need through market intelligence and consumer research. Taking care to remember that what consumers need is often not what they say they want. As automotive pioneer Henry Ford once observed: 'If we had asked customers what they wanted, they would have said a faster horse.'

Companies will always struggle to meet self-imposed deadlines and keep promises that have no additional value for the customer. Why have a policy to return a customer's call within 30 minutes if customers are willing to wait two hours? You make enormous efforts to hit, and often miss, that 30-minute deadline. Even though customers don't require it, and plainly didn't ask you for it.

Why set your brand up for failure by trying to meet unnecessarily high customer expectations? Overpromising always sounds good in Marketing meetings. If you look today, I'll bet you can find an area of your company where you are overpromising. If you are, please stop it. Scale back your ambitions. Look for areas that require a great deal of time and effort like round-the-clock customer service; personal meetings; tailor-made additional functionality – and simply wind back some of your aspirations. Promising beyond market need creates unnecessary work for your employees and unwanted angst for your management team.

Is this an appeal for mediocrity? No, it is not. It is a suggestion that we could be more pragmatic about goal setting. Then we might get around to pleasing our customers rather more often. My advice is to go big on vision, but be realistic about goals.

First published May 2014

▶ Branding Tip 5 – try Marketing frugally

Earlier in this chapter, I talked about the universal aspiration to brand leadership. If you decide to pursue it, the good news is that it won't always require an enormous Marketing budget. There's often a path to success that doesn't require you to splash the cash.

Here's a nice example from the global beer category. They say that beer brands are all about image, but that image doesn't always have to be super premium. Yes, a segment of consumers will always be attracted by the promise 'reassuringly expensive'. But in beer, as in many other spheres of brand activity, lower cost offerings have higher volume appeal.

Oettinger Brauerei is a popular brewing group in Germany. Since 2004, when it overtook sales of Krombacher, Oettinger has been Germany's best-selling beer brand, with an annual volume of over 6.6 million hectolitres. That's enough to fuel plenty of singing, sideways marching, and truly Teutonic hangovers.

Oettinger sells large amounts of beer for the lowest possible price. It is rarely found on tap in pubs and bars, as most of it is sold in bottles from supermarkets. Oettinger uses several strategies to keep its beer prices low. For a start, Oettinger does not advertise. Nor does Oettinger use distribution intermediaries, preferring to use its own branded trucks to deliver directly to stores. And the brewing process is highly automated, using very few employees to brew vast quantities of beer.

In the automotive sector, the Tata Nano, the world's cheapest car, had become a symbolic brand long before the first one rolled off the production line in 2009. The Tata Group hyped it as the forerunner of a new revolution. A movement of frugal innovation that would put consumer products within reach of ordinary Indians and Chinese. Tata claimed that the cost savings would be so huge that a new generation of frugal ideas would conquer the world.

Alas, the plucky little car was dogged with problems from the start. Protesting farmers forced Tata Motors to move production out of one Indian state and into another. Early sales drives failed to catch fire, but some of the cars literally did. So, was frugal innovation being oversold, and can Western manufacturing giants now relax?

Two new books, "Reverse Innovation" by Vijay Govindarajan and Chris Trimble, and "Jugaad Innovation" by Navi Radjou, Jaideep Prabhu and Simone Ahuja suggest that answer to both questions is a definitive 'no'. Instead, both these publications show that frugal innovation is flourishing across the emerging world, despite the gurus' failure to agree on a term to describe it. They also argue that it will change rich countries in due course.

Predictably. some multinationals are beginning to take ideas developed in the emerging world and deploy them in the West. Harman, an American company that makes infotainment systems for cars, developed a new system for emerging markets (dubbed Saras from the Sanskrit word for flexible) using a simpler design and Asian engineering. Toyota is now a major customer. China's Haier has undercut Western competitors in a wide range of products, from air conditioners and washing machines to wine coolers. Haier sells a wine cooler for half the price of the brand leader, and has grabbed 60% of the US market in just two years.

The West is doomed to a long period of austerity, as the middle class is squeezed and governments curb spending. Spain and Portugal will soon join Italy and Greece in the deepening Euro crisis. Meanwhile, at 25%, Spain's unemployment rate is the same as South Africa's. The millions of affected consumers will soon be crying out for new ways to save money. So, the trend to frugality looks set to accelerate.

A growing list of Western Universities are also taking this new message to heart. Santa Clara University has a Frugal Innovation Lab. Stanford University has an Entrepreneurial Design for Extreme Affordability programme (kudos for the snappy title, guys). And even good old Cambridge University has an Inclusive Design programme.

So, if frugality is being deployed in product design, perhaps it is time that Marketers were cleverer with their pennies. When these ground-breaking innovations are ready to go to market, let's see some real innovation in messaging and digital frugality in channel mix.

First published July 2013

**Brand Manager
urgently sought**

Every other chapter in this book gives me the opportunity to profile an East African Marketing professional whom I admire.

Almost every one of them was a Brand Manager in their early careers. All of them understand branding very well, and have influenced many of the brands that we have grown up with in Africa.

But when we turned our collective minds to the Brand Managers of today, we struggled to identify candidates to promote.

For this reason, we decided to run an ad here instead.

BRAND MANAGER

We're looking for a real Brand Manager whose career we can promote.

You must be resident in East Africa, and in full time employment as a Brand Manager.

Once you have read every chapter in this book, you'll know the kind of qualities we are looking for. But what it really boils down to is this:

- Have you made a measurable impact on the performance of a brand?

We're not too bothered about your academic qualifications:

- We're more interested in your attitude towards building brands.
- We'd like to know whether your colleagues from other disciplines rate you.
- We'll be very interested in the proof of efficacy you choose to submit.

So, submit your application letter and supporting documents without delay* to:

marketingmedicine2019@gmail.com

A wider world of opportunity awaits you.

*Read the book first. All of it.

Chapter 2

Setting Strategy

If you've just completed Chapter One of this book, you must be enthusiastic about the world of Brand Management. Perhaps you own or lead a company that employs Marketers, and you're curious to know how they spend their time. Perhaps you're a young Marketer who has read all the textbooks but now faces commercial reality.

Rather too many modern Marketers get distracted by activity. By making things happen, and by spending company money. They forget that their colleagues and employers are actually looking for productivity.

One the most important tasks for any competent Brand Manager is to develop a Marketing strategy. Not every day, of course, but certainly at the start of each year. And the best way to write a strategy is to begin with the end in mind. Identifying the desired results of your Marketing activities; and setting measures in place to assess return on investment.

While brand awareness and preference are important to success, most people in the business will want to see hard commercial returns. Increased customer base, frequency of purchase, additional volume stimulated and maintained by promotional activity. Any Marketer would be foolish to ignore such opportunities for validation. Marketing is a business activity; not an academic or artistic pastime.

In this chapter, we discuss how to frame strategy to deliver successful Marketing campaigns.

Strategy starts with results

In Kampala recently, I heard the amusing tale of how one of Uganda's many mobile networks came to be. Apparently, the Middle Eastern owners heard that the Southern Sudan telecoms market was about to open up. So, they left their glass tower in the Gulf and flew by executive jet to Juba. At the time, Juba was a dusty pre-medieval city, where foreigners were suspect and accommodation for investors was decidedly flea-bitten. After a short tour the perfumed gentlemen were so horrified that they jumped back into their jet and ordered the pilot to fly them to the nearest place of civilisation. That place was Uganda, where their spirits were restored by several nights carousing in Kampala.

They decided to invest and, some months later, they launched their mobile phone network. Using their resources in the Gulf they spent an eye-watering amount of money on a TV campaign, intended to attract high spending Ugandans to a premium-priced, VIP network. The campaign ran for less than a month. Then the gentlemen returned to review progress and were disappointed. They decided to switch the network's brand promise to a value for money offering for the 'Bottom of the Pyramid'. But a brand needs to choose a customer type and remain true to them. Brands are built over time, and not in the first flush of enthusiasm. The network failed to find traction.

The story reminds me how random so many business decisions seem to be. How subjective and inward looking. Especially, it seems, decisions about Marketing. It sometimes seems that anyone can be a Marketer. Often, it's the people furthest removed from the consumer who are most excited by the opportunity to dabble. Recently I read a leading global PR practitioner discussing the problem of clients re-writing her press releases. She described them as 'floundering in the shallow end' of communications.

Professional Marketers and their Agencies have a responsibility to bring order to this chaos. Their mission should start and end with the consumer (sometimes called the target audience). And it should specify a desired behaviour change. Because that is what Marketing does: it shapes attitudes and behaviours, which in turn make sales and revenue growth easier.

Professional Marketers like to get to grips with results. Take the impact of advertising as an example. Yes, it can be hard to link advertising effort directly to sales, because of the other variables in the sales mix. But it isn't impossible. What it needs is for the Marketing team and their advisors to agree a set of criteria. And commit to a method of measurement.

This could be a simple econometric model. It could be a measurement of store traffic, or promotion entries, or publicity coverage. But it needs to be something, and it needs to be agreed up front. Otherwise, all parties charge off down the path of execution and forget where they started. And then, when the campaign is over, they try to hurry on to the next one without pausing to take stock.

I visit a lot of Advertising Agencies, and I like to see their case studies. Their examples of how great ideas changed behaviours and produced business results. I see some truly great work, and I get a general impression of effectiveness. But I cannot tell you how often we come to the results section of the case study only to hear: 'Ah, the client was very pleased with the campaign' or 'Yes, the campaign was very popular.' When I ask for something more tangible, I am often told: 'The client was not prepared to share results because of business confidentiality.' This makes no sense to me. Good business people seek proof, and are proud to showcase achievement.

In Kenya, the lack of consensus on Marketing results has led Procurement people and senior management to think that media buying discounts are the primary measure of a campaign's effectiveness. Because that seems tangible and 'balance sheet' measureable. 'We are satisfied that our Marketing team struck a deal to buy media very cheaply.' Even in the days when people claimed that the medium was the message, such one-dimensional thinking would have been questioned.

If you are dissatisfied with your latest Marketing campaign, the chances are you began it without a clear consensus on the desired result.

First published June 2011

Be clear on your business purpose

When you look at the East African region, there are no more than fifteen serious business categories driving our economies. In some of our markets all categories are represented, in others there may be one dominant player and less than half a dozen competitors. To be honest, that's not really competitive.

Yet in some key sectors, Regulators have already failed us. Particularly those whose duty is to restrain the giants. Restrain does not mean punish, restrain means apply a touch on the brakes when it looks like Bank A or Telecoms Company B or Advertising Agency C is running away with the market. But perhaps East African monopolies and competition watch dogs are looking in the wrong direction. Dazzled by the legal muscle, the financial canniness or whatever other distractions the biggest enterprises in our region can array. I saw in the papers yesterday that Kenya has just hosted a global forum on anti-competitive behaviour. I'll be looking to see if anything meaningful emerges from that.

Weak restraints on anti-competitive positions don't bother small companies or niche brands very much. Small companies don't steal – or borrow – market share. More often they create more choices; new capabilities; new franchises. They define for themselves a very clear business purpose. Small companies know that, if they try to compete on the same terms as the big boys, they will lose. So, as consultancy **www.londonstrategyunit.com** always asks: 'Why play their game when you can invent your own? Small companies should create and capture new markets. Rather than copying incumbents, they will thrive by meeting unmet needs.'

By contrast, mid-sized brands that lack a true purpose are the most vulnerable to competitive threats. There are plenty of them in our region. Some are reforming after years of traditional management; many are family businesses going through generation change. Some are former parastatals. Most have been poorly branded. By this I don't mean that you don't know them, or wouldn't recognise their logos. I mean that they are stuck in the middle ground between brand leaders and niche (specialised) brands. Which means that consumers don't really care whether they thrive or perish.

Brands stuck in the middle ground tend to fight battles on all fronts in an attempt to stay relevant. They may try to hold on to both ends of their categories: simultaneously dropping prices while trying to creating more premium offerings. I see it all the time in the Marketing briefs they write: 'Engage with urban youth without alienating rural middle class' or 'This brand was male-focused, but is now appealing to both genders.' Unfortunately, when you're competing on all sides, it's easy to forget your original business purpose. If this is your company's situation, take a moment to ask yourself why your brand deserves to exist – over and above the need to make a profit.

You may be surprised to hear that the social media brand Twitter is a good example of a company that got quite big... and then got lost. With the arrival of new platforms like Snapchat and Vine, Twitter has realised that it no longer offers users a compelling reason to use. Is Twitter for news or for chats? For networking or for stirring up political dissent? Realising how important it is to have business purpose, Twitter went and asked its Twitterers to **#describetwitterin3words**. Most of those words were unwelcome, but at least they gave Twitter something to work on. 'I don't know' was pretty popular, as was 'needs less stalkers.'

Unlike Twitter, plenty of mid-sized brands haven't yet realised that they've lost their true purpose and therefore their place in consumers' lives. So, very helpfully, LSU has given us three symptoms of purposeless to look out for:

1. *Purposeless companies work in silos.* Without a unifying purpose, departments tend to hunker down and just get on with doing their day job, whatever that might be. What is clear is that their job has nothing much to do with anyone else's. Companies with a clear purpose are the opposite. Teams join up across silos to achieve a shared goal: delivering on a business purpose that is much bigger than the agenda of any one department.

2. *Purposeless companies do everything, yet prioritise nothing.* Companies with purpose have a 'not to-do list'. They make sacrifices because they know certain things distract from their core business purpose. Too many companies think offering affordability, quality, authenticity, convenience and great service is their purpose – which basically signals 'we offer everything, but are expert at nothing'.

3. *Purposeless companies navigate by the competition.* The phrase 'It worked for them' is an obvious symptom of a company without a business purpose. It's all too easy to react to every new market trend with the justification: "it worked for someone else, so it'll work for us, right?" Rather than living in a state of knee-jerk reaction, purpose-driven organisations create and capture new markets they can dominate. They would rather be the first to spot and serve an unmet consumer need than desperately defend their share of a declining market.

This all makes sense to me, and it rings very true in East Africa. So, if you recognise any of the above traits in your brand or business, it's probably time to refresh your approach. Go back to your business purpose and work harder on it. Then share it with your staff, so that they can understand and deliver it.

First published August 2015

Seek Out the Catalytic Idea

A successful Marketing strategy should always be based on a strong commercial idea. We all have ideas. In meetings; in bars; in the bath. Talking with friends; networking for business. But the trouble is that few of them produce significant changes to life or business. At best, they make incremental shifts.

I have a habit of placing Post-It pads around my house and in my car. I use them to capture ideas. The best ideation times for me are after exercise, or upon waking. But if I don't note them down quickly they are gone. No amount of Ginseng or Fish Oil seems to alter that.

A great many of my ideas (and yours) are what we call isolic. They are the smart ideas that raise a smile when you have them. And, if you action them, they produce a short-term fix or improvement. They are important to have, but their effects are not long-lived. They are not ideas that make people think new thoughts, or act in very different ways.

When I look at modern Marketing campaigns, I realise that most Marketing ideas are isolic. They produce gradual improvement at best. That's why some Marketers move company every two years; before the downturns occasioned by their actions become noticeable.

But many companies inch forward by producing a high volume of isolic ideas. Anita Roddick, who founded successful retailer The Body Shop admitted that: 'What we needed was an avalanche of ideas that kept us separate from the competition.' She realised that one aspect of her brand's differentiation was constant innovation. Small changes, that built an overall perception of progress.

Innovation as a word ranks high in the Marketer's Lexicon. I run brand workshops all the time. The temptation to sneak the word 'innovative' into a description of brand character seems overwhelming. But sadly, very few brands, and even fewer Brand Managers, are truly innovative. They are at best active, and they hope in good faith that this activity will produce results. There's little consideration here of qualitative change. The change that can be created by better, bigger ideas.

Fortunately, there is another kind of idea. It's a rarer animal altogether. The kind of idea that produces a step change – in a business, in a market, in a civilisation. For that reason, we call it catalytic. Here is a non-Marketing example. In 1917 the German national leadership was in despair. They had been fighting the Russians for three long years of attrition and stalemate. Then one of their number shared a suggestion with his colleagues. He believed he had discovered a weapon more powerful than any used before. A weapon that would strike well beyond the Russian front line, and even impact on their cities in the rear. That weapon was not a bomb, it was an idea.

The idea existed in the mind of a Russian exile living in Germany. So, the leaders invited him to Berlin. And then they put him on a train to Moscow. Upon his arrival, this man began to spread the idea. Within months, the idea had spread to the Russian trenches, and caused two million soldiers to leave their posts. The Moscow war machine ground to a halt. Then the idea spread and riots engulfed the cities. Eventually the Government fell. The date was November 1917. The idea was Communism, and the man on the train was Lenin.

Let's all spend more time evaluating the impact of catalytic ideas on Marketing and business.

First published March 2010

Think bigger

We now understand ideas, and can separate them into two camps. First, the isolic idea. The clever notion your friends all applaud, but forget within a week. The incremental idea that inches your brand forwards rather than producing a significant leap forwards. Then there's the game-changer: the catalytic idea. A thought so motivating that it changes the way people think and behave.

The Internet is swamped with no-brain or low-brain suggestions for Marketing action. The worst thing about looking for ideas on the Web is that it benchmarks you against the past. Very rarely do great ideas appear like a Biblical vision: perfect in form, unquestionable, inspiring. Generally, they need discussion, challenging and building upon. And sometimes they just need rubbishing.

Google '100 best Marketing ideas' and you enter a colourless land. Here Sam Hczk, of Affordable Insurance, jostles for position with Mari Kisckynski of Red Hot MBA Reading. (Who are these people, and why are there so many consonants in their names?)

A little further on you may encounter '80 best Guerrilla Marketing ideas'. There's some useable stuff in here, but everything is isolic. Quick win, big splash, over and done with.

By contrast, initial sales of the electric toothbrush were driven by a catalytic Marketing idea. The device itself was not a breakthrough. The electric toothbrush has been around since the 1950's, but for decades was a niche product. In research, consumers admitted it was convenient, but looked down on it as a lazy person's appliance. Then someone came up with the idea that while ordinary toothbrushes remove food debris, only the electric toothbrush could remove plaque. So, they put that in their Marketing campaign, and on their packaging. They got the dental profession to endorse it. Then, hey presto, consumers stopped thinking about electric toothbrushes as labour-saving appliances, and began to consider the healthcare benefits.

Now that is a catalytic idea. And it won't have been developed in isolation. It comes from a time when marketers, production people, finance people, and outside advisors like advertising or PR agents sat down and talked. They talked collaboratively, and they explored possibilities. They probably had fun doing it.

Collaborative action by clever people produces most of the world's catalytic ideas. Working together on the same intellectual agenda also allows groups to make mistakes and to learn from them. Legendary thinker Edward de Bono placed emphasis on the importance of permitting ideas to fail, as the basis for the emergence of better ideas. For African markets to bloom we need more intelligent collaboration, and cleverer people in Marketing. And we need to stop looking at Marketing advisors as people we pay for on a cost-plus basis. Cheap fees mean cheap people on the business. Cheap people on the business mean fewer great ideas.

Leading London Advertising Agency, Rainey Kelly Campbell Roalfe, made its name and fortune by charging clients for the value of the ideas they created. It's rumoured that they charged UK retailer Marks & Spencer one million Sterling Pounds for the "My M&S" idea that changed the brand's business fortunes. No messing about with media commissions or cost of resource plus an agreed profit margin there! And everyone, starting with the M&S customer, was happier for it.

First published April 2010

Strategy: Stick to it.

There are many tools and processes available to leadership teams who want to strategise. Sometimes I think there are too many, and I'm always of the opinion that the simplest models are the best. Too many questions to answer, too many options to expound and your strategic plan soon becomes an end rather than a means.

But there's one thing harder than coming up with a winning strategy ... and that's sticking to it. Whether it's the five-year plan for your business or the three-year plan for your brand. The temptation to tinker starts as soon as the ink is dry. It's hard to resist; harder still if the First Quarter's results aren't what you had hoped for. Or if your CFO meets a new consultant whose sales talk makes the current plan seem shoddy. Or there's a change of leadership in the business. But here's what happens if you don't stick to your plan.

First of all, the employees, to whom you 'sold' the strategy in the first place, begin to ask questions. The first question they will ask is: 'Does my boss really know what she's doing?' This is understandable, because employees like bosses who set a clear direction and explain the role each of them has to play. They like that almost as much as they dislike change. For change always means more work, and often provokes internal conflict.

Secondly, your business partners start to roll their eyes. Your strategic partners in retail or logistics or packaging, or whatever intimate support your business requires for success, who went out of their way to accommodate your intentions into their own plans. This is a problem, because you want your partners to be your promoters. To actively endorse your strategy, products and services to other parties in the business community. Not to say: 'We just don't know what Company A is up to anymore.'

Thirdly, and most alarmingly, your customers become puzzled. Customers are very quick to perceive a change of direction and easily become unsettled. Indeed, if you are fortunate to have created a really popular brand, you may find customers actively opposing a change in strategy. This is because brands belong to consumers more than they belong to brand owners; they exist in the hearts and minds of the people who buy them.

So, against this backdrop, I have been delighted to reconnect recently with a couple of brands that have stuck to their strategy.

Seven years ago, I was privileged to work with a company that started life as a tyre dealer in Western Kenya. They had built a good business in partnership with Pirelli (which continues to this day) but they felt there was an opportunity to enjoy brand success independent of that global giant. Together we worked on a strategy to launch the brand that was to become known as AutoXpress **www.auto-xpress.co.ke**

One pillar of that strategy was the requirement to create highly visible, modern tyre centres. They stuck to their plan, and now boast 29 outlets in Kenya, Tanzania and Rwanda. More importantly, they executed their brand identity to exactly the same standard in every location. This is much harder than it sounds – thanks to the human propensity to express individuality. Just look at what employees do to their business card design if given the leeway to make changes.

And now the AutoXpress team is extending that discipline to the digital space – enabling customers to specify, cost and compare, and book appointments to fit a wide range of auto accessories. They are also line-extending the brand into much more capable auto-repair centres in partnership with global brand leader Bosch. All of which represents innovation – but innovation in line with the original strategy.

The other day I was back on the ranch, re-engaging with a brand called Mara Beef. **www.marabeef.com**

This brand is still in the early stages of its journey, but the young owners have remained true to the strategic principles we agreed nearly three years ago. They are adding value; in terms of more educated cattle husbandry, a modern abattoir and tasty processed beef product development. Their vehicles and packaging bear a simple, strong logo that connotes healthy grass-fed beef on the range. They have enlisted the local community, and are rewarding its support with training, development and business opportunities. In this way, Mara Beef is laying the foundations of a food brand we may all come to admire as it develops in scale, communicates with its target audiences... and above all sticks to its strategy.

First published June 2016

Here are 5 tips to help you create winning strategies:

▶ Strategy Tip 1 – drop the bull

It's often good to pause and remind yourself of the basics of any profession. I am sure that zealous dentists from time to time give themselves a jolly good talking-to about their approach to the humble filling. Accountants may take down their double entry book for a spot of concentrated bookkeeping. Commercial pilots spend weeks every year in simulators practicing the little things that make a difference in everyday flight and save lives during crises.

It should be the same with brand strategy. And where better to start than reminding ourselves what a brand actually is? It's not complicated – although some of our more bullish Marketers may portray it as such – but neither is it easy. In simple terms a brand is a value proposition you construct for ... well, almost anything. Your granny is a brand, banks have brands, and there are brands in medicine and education. There are branded law firms, although perhaps not thanks to any conscious process. In my time, I have branded antiretroviral drug therapy for HIV, driving instructors, game conservancies and even electricity.

The value is created when you combine a function with an emotion. McDonalds began serving food without cutlery to save costs, but made their counter service fast and peppy. They laid out their restaurants to be ergonomically efficient. This produced customer gratitude for fast and convenient service. 'Thank you,' said diners, 'we don't have to waste time being served by a surly waitress at her speed. We can eat at our speed.' McDonalds was not about delicious food.

Colgate is the world's best-selling toothpaste brand. I'm not sure it cleans your teeth a whole lot better than other pastes, but it had a breakthrough moment when it decided to own the notion of Social Confidence. Those clever Marketers at Colgate worked out that fresh breath boosted personal confidence, and was even more appealing than having white or cavity free teeth. Here in Africa, we validated that truth right at the bottom of society, where people who buy the smallest tubes of Colgate use it on Sunday – the most sociable day of the week.

In service brands, the emotional dimension is best conveyed by staff behaviours, often expressed as 'the way we do it around here'. In this weekend's Sunday Times, I read about Sir Richard Branson's latest extension of his Virgin brand. Virgin Hotels has just opened in Chicago and an estate of some 150 city properties is planned. The first hotel is straight out the Virgin brand book – it takes away all the things that annoy you about city hotels, adds British humour, international style and a dash of sex. Just to be clear, that does not mean that sex is on offer at Virgin Hotels. However, Virgin has patented a new kind of bed – the lounge bed – upon which you can stretch out and read or work comfortably, or do something more adventurous.

Check-in is online, and your room key pops out of a machine at Reception when you scan your QR code. In your room you control the audio, TV, climate and Room Service via your mobile phone or tablet. There's no extra charge for Room Service: the items in your red Smeg mini fridge are at retail prices. 'Why would I charge someone $3 for a Snickers bar and piss them off so much that they never come back?' asks Sir Richard. And it's a good ask.

The Virgin brand has a mission to be egalitarian and fun. So, the private members bar in the hotel is actually open to everyone and is accordingly called The Commons in a nod to British parliamentary history. And, as almost half the business travellers in the US are ladies, public areas are softly lit ... while bathrooms have brightly lit vanity mirrors and showers with benches, which make it easier to shave your legs.

People often say to me that the logo is the brand, but it really isn't. Any more than changing your bank from yellow to black is a rebranding. The logo should be the simplest graphic identifier you wish to associate with your brand. Think Nike tick. A logo's job is not to tell the brand story, but to signal that the brand is present.

Branding began with the ownership of livestock, probably millennia ago. At that time, farmers quickly learnt that cutting a deliberate mark on their cattle's haunches would make them easy to recognise. That mark would make appropriating a cow a deliberate act of theft. It was a mark of ownership.

Later, when some herders got better at rearing cattle, people in the marketplace (literally the cattle market) would get to notice that cows with the specific brand marks were fatter and glossier. So, the mark became a signal of value, and bidders would pay more for cows with specific brands. Interestingly our modern understanding of monetary value originates from the time when our fortunes depended on success in the livestock market. The word impecunious comes from the Ancient Greek word for cattle. If you were without cattle, you were without wealth. A concept any Maasai would readily understand.

So, when you want to remind yourself about the fundamentals of the brand building process, think cows. Not bull.

First published January 2015

▶ Strategy Tip 2 – define your brand belief

Never underestimate the importance of mainstream consumers in any society. The good people who conform; who value security; who don't rock the boat. They are the audience most consumer brands yearn for, but they are hard to recruit. Their resistance to new ideas makes them reluctant adopters of new brand offerings.

To overcome mainstreamer resistance, a Marketer must fast track the task of making his brand familiar and accepted in the shortest possible time. Great distribution helps this; Coca-Cola has long had a mission to get an ice-cold Coke within arm's reach of as many people has possible. Wrigley's has invested many 'man years' and millions of dollars streamlining the flow of products down to kiosk level. South African Breweries, long before they were SABMiller, were first and foremost an incredibly efficient distribution machine.

Widespread consumer engagement activity is also necessary. In rural villages and urban neighbourhoods; at churches, malls and places of assembly. These interactions help consumers to recognise and handle the product; taste it and talk about it. Advertising and brand PR also have their role to play in making a new brand look established. And when it comes to advertising you might think that the best way to accelerate a brand's acceptance is to spend more money in media. But that's only true up to a point.

The real truth is that, if your brand does not stand for something simple, relevant and enduring, it will take a very long time to become accepted. I have lost count of the manufacturers I have met in Africa who have devoted their lives to producing the best quality jam, tea, margarine or shock absorbers. Yet invested very little time in understanding the quality those consumers will happily accept (which may be lower). Or the consumer need that their brand might address. For many leading manufacturers, it is enough that they have strived for quality, and the consumer should jolly well be prepared to pay for it! They become a little outraged if consumer demand is anything less than massive.

I'm a passionate advocate for brands having a central belief, a clear reason for being that forms the core of any activity or communication the brand carries out. The strongest brands on the globe have evolved a Brand Belief, which has two components. Firstly, an Ideology, which describes a point of view on the world that defines the opportunity for the brand. Secondly a Statement of Intent, quite literally 'what the brand intends to do about it'. Allow me to illustrate:

- **Virgin**

  Ideology: Virgin believes that big, faceless corporations abuse the interests of ordinary people.

  Statement of Intent: Virgin champions the rights of the consumers by challenging the established rules of the category, and has fun so doing.

  (When you read this, you begin to understand why Virgin Mobile ads talk the way they do, or why the service on-board Virgin Atlantic is more relaxed and light-hearted than on more formal airlines.)

- **Disney**

  Ideology: Disney believes everyone should hold onto his or her childhood imagination.

  Statement of Intent: Disney designs fantasies that offer magical experiences to people of all ages

  (Thus, the development of the Disney product range, which runs from movies to theme parks to toys, is set in a context that is more easily understood.)

- **The Olympic Games**.

  Ideology: The Olympics Games believes that competitive spirit is Humanity's most powerful unifying force.

  Statement of Intent: The Olympic Games brings the world together in the pursuit of excellence.

Now, these enterprises may not have begun with a written-down Brand Belief. But they did begin with an idea, often in the mind of the single individual who created the business. And, as they developed their products and services, they have tried to remain true to that original idea.

But what is stopping us, here and now in Africa, from short-cutting this process? If you are a brand owner, and you suspect your brand may not have a belief, please do this. Take a pen and a piece of paper and write down your Ideology and Statement of Intent. I'm willing to bet that this will make things clearer for you, for your staff and for your customers.

First published August 2011

▶ Strategy Tip 3 – prioritise likeability

I turned off a movie last night, long before it had finished playing. That's the modern equivalent of walking out of a cinema early, which I have only done twice in my life. Once was during a screening of 'Natural Born Killers', a desolate portrayal of young people who kill for kicks. And the other time was fifteen minutes into a screening of 'Invasion Earth' which turned out to be a dramatisation of L. Ron Hubbard's explanation of how we humans came to be. I went in hoping for laser-charged dogfights but got loony Scientologists John Travolta and Forrest Whitaker clomping around in space suits with platform heels, dreadlocks and nose plugs.

I turned off the movie 'Chef' after giving it a good hour of my time. I pushed the button because I could not empathise with any aspect of the film or connect with a single character. An obnoxious chef gets fired by an even more obnoxious restaurant owner (played by Dustin Hoffman) and sets off with his neglected son and loyal sous chef to run a food truck. On the way, they learn about the power of Twitter. If I had watched till the end I expect that they would all have ended up weeping and hugging. The Chef would have returned home to the delight of his wife and son. The restaurant owner would have rehired him, and the restaurant critic who caused the dismissal might well have experienced a Damascene conversion.

Movies and TV shows are brands. Indeed, for many years the crime series CSI was the most powerful brand in the US, on a range of commercial measures. Shows like this are volatile brands because their functional delivery (entertainment/education) is surpassed by their emotional impact. As with any brand, their ability to be liked and admired is a major determinant of revenue. And the box office provides an immediate, public and unequivocal measure of brand success.

In Marketing language, I rejected 'Chef' because I felt no brand affinity. As a result, I did not conclude my transaction with the brand. Nor would I be open to line extension (Chef 2: Return of the Critic) or to any other work featuring the actor Jon Favreau, who played the eponymous cook. Nor will my contribution to word of mouth be positive – watch my Twitter feed to see life imitating art.

I've spent the intervening 24 hours thinking about the brands in my life and outside it. I lack affinity with Mercedes, Barclays Bank, Greece, Safaricom, Jack Black, Arsenal and Castle Lager. That does not mean I actively dislike them, but I am not predisposed towards them. Even when they offer something that could fit into my life, they don't make it onto the long list.

On the other hand, I do have affinity with the following brands. And the reasons for the connections between us are varied. I like McDonalds, because their breakfast offering is just perfect when you are on the move. I associate the Egg & Bacon McMuffin with early mornings on the road in the European winter. I support Toyota because I have actually driven off-road, and the Landcruiser 4WD fills me with confidence. I use MPESA because it is convenient and inclusive. I fly Virgin Atlantic, when I can, because it turns air travel into stylish fun. I brush with Colgate because I have done since I was a child – and find it clean and wholesome. I meet and eat at Art Caffé because the nature of the service is as desirable as the food. I drink Windhoek Light because it's the best tasting low alcohol beer I have ever supped, and I find its German brewing heritage reassuring.

I've just received the latest annual from Superbrands East Africa. It's the product of an initiative I am pleased to support. Page through it and you will find brands of many hues, and you'll register a different reaction to each. But you'll know in your heart which brands you have affinity with. Brand affinity. Considerably more valuable than brand awareness.

First published September 2014

▶ Strategy Tip 4 – set brand energy

Marketers love jargon, don't they? Most of the time you have no idea what they are talking about. Sometimes they have no idea either. Jargon binds groups together in a self-satisfied way. Stockbrokers talk about PE ratios, CFOs talk about EBITDA, and lawyers talk about 'tag along, drag along.' I am sure nuclear physicists have a secret language but I'm too tired to find out, after talking to all those lawyers and stockbrokers. I also have a good friend in the sugar industry – so I know much more about the jargon in that business than is strictly healthy.

Jargon is a defensive weapon, a barricade used to exclude others and to obfuscate difficult issues. So, it won't surprise you to hear that I am profoundly anti-jargon. When I hear expressions like Unique Selling Proposition my jaw begins to clench. Not because the intention is wrong, but because in 95% of cases the outcome is going to be anodyne and predictable. This is because defining a brand's uniqueness is very hard to do from inside the factory, or the bank, or the telecoms head office.

And yet consumers refuse to let business commoditise itself completely. Brands still mean things – sometimes great things – to the people who buy them. Strong brands continue to command their desired price point through thick and thin. Strong corporate brands generate higher shareholder value. That's a fact.

People often gravitate towards brands that radiate a certain energy. But the funny thing is, very few Marketers ever think about energy when they make plans for their brands. Perhaps energy is hard to define; less tangible than taste preference or customer satisfaction scores. Perhaps because no one has ever tried to measure brand energy. Until now.

Recently Professor Robert Jacobson of University of Washington Business School, and Professor Natalie Mizik of Columbia Business School cracked the problem. They sampled data from BrandAssetValuator™ (the world's largest database of brand health). Then they crossed it with Standard & Poor's Compustat data tapes for accounting performance measures, and factored in data from the University of Chicago's Centre for Research in Security Prices. To cut a long story short, they reviewed many top brands that are listed on the New York Stock Exchange: Disney, Coca-Cola, Apple, McDonalds and so on. They examined their stock performance over time against the power of their brand imagery. And they came up with a precise mathematical formula for brand energy.

I don't have access to that formula, as it is proprietary. But, in plain English, brand energy is a perception that a brand is moving in a particular direction, and has a clear purpose in the world. Now just think about that for a minute. Think about the many brands you know (if you are a CEO, think about your own brand) and ask yourself if you can describe the direction in which it is moving, and its purpose in the world. Not your Company, your brand.

It's surprisingly difficult, but I'll give you a hint. Unless you really understand what consumers think and feel about your brand, you will be wide of the mark.

First published November 2010

▶ Strategy Tip 5 – feel your brand pulse

US academics have just made breakthroughs in measuring brand energy. They went on to identify those aspects of a brand that appear to drive higher energy levels. They named them Vision, Invention and Dynamism. And finally, they ranked NYSE listed brands by scoring them from 0-100 on a model too clever to explain in this short space. In the end, they were able to group brands into seven energy levels.

The top level was Volcanic. A CEO with a such brand is the commercial equivalent of a top-flight US Marine. A man or woman of action; prepared to take risks; bright and brave enough to wrong foot the opposition. But what of the six other levels? Let's review, and then let's conduct an exercise that enables you to place your brand within its competitive context, in terms of the energy created.

Level 1: *Volcanic*. You've got the idea, right?

Level 2: *Burning*. Your brand is as hot as a pili-pili chicken at Nandos. Consumers feel its heat. You've come a long way, but you still haven't quite learned how to live in the spotlight. It's time to do something that pushes your brand up to the ultimate level. Brands in this position may have a window as tight as two years to make the leap. Starbucks was here once. So was Viagra. So was Myspace. In East Africa, most of our ISPs were here two years ago.

Level 3: *Charged*. Your brand is being noticed. It's moving in the right direction. It is liked and purchased repeatedly by loyal consumers. Now is the time to figure out how to get it into the mass consciousness. So, think outside the confines of your market segment, and beyond the functional delivery of your brand. How can you give it greater social relevance? Coke did this in the 1930's when they gave Santa a Coca-Cola red coat and moved the brand from summer refreshment to all-year-round fizzy drink icon. (St. Nicholas had traditionally always worn green.)

Level 4: *Pulsing*. Well, at least your brand has a pulse. This is a condition in which we find many brands in Africa. Market share gain is positive; profitability is good. Which is why most CEOs and CFOs stop pushing for more. But this is where a good Brand Manager can make all the difference. It is her job to keep driving more Invention and Dynamism into her brand. McDonalds was making good money offering meat in a bun at a low price, but they went on to add fun: Happy Meals, birthday parties and a rather scary clown. More recently they have added health. McDonalds' brand energy is now volcanic.

Level 5: *Inert*. In Africa, we have far too many brands in this category. They are named products, not real brands. In this group, Brand Manager creativity has been exhausted by developing straplines like 'We care for you!' and they have turned their attention to scamming money from suppliers of Marketing services. Admittedly some of these brands are in low interest categories. But, so what? In the unspeakably dull computer components sector, Intel has become an iconic brand. If they can do it, so can you. But you have to want to.

Level 6: *Sleeping*. This is the starting point for many new brands in Africa. A name, a logo and ... nothing more. A brand in this state needs sound professional advice on targeting and differentiation. Get these wrong, and it'll never have a pulse. 'If you ain't segmenting,' said Theodore Levitt of Harvard Business School, 'you ain't Marketing.'

Level 7. *Decaying*. Here's the good news. I doubt we have many brands in this state in Africa. We haven't been going long enough for this to happen. However, as expertise in branding becomes more established, decay will become a future challenge. Elsewhere in the world, decayed food brands are being exterminated by supermarket own labels. If a whole category falls into decay, it becomes vulnerable to competitors like Sir Richard Branson, whose skill is to reinvent an industry in his own image. So, watch out for this from our future entrepreneurs.

Now to the exercise. To see where any brand sits in terms of the brand energy it exudes, choose a category (let's say, for example, restaurants). Take a piece of paper or create a spreadsheet. Along the X-Axis write the names of all the restaurant brands you can think of, and on the Y-Axis write the seven categories described above. Then, without thinking too hard, because intuitive responses are more accurate, plot your perception of energy level of each brand.

Then take a look at the picture you have created and try to summarise why you feel the better performing brands seem have more energy. Here's a clue – think about Vision, Invention and Dynamism.

First published December 2010

Let's meet a
Strategic Star

Marion Gathoga-Mwangi

Marion Gathoga-Mwangi was educated at United States International University, Africa. She began her Marketing career with Nestlé in Kenya as a Product Specialist on Foods. Since then she has steadily climbed the corporate ladder in major multinational and regional companies in Africa. Division Manager at Bayer; Sales and Marketing Director with AMSCO; Country Director Kenya and East Africa at Cadbury (Mondelez International); General Manager of Unga Group; Country Manager Botswana for Parmalat. She is currently the Managing Director of BOC Kenya (Linde Group).

Her category experience is obviously rich and varied: from consumer goods to industrial manufacturing. Marion is an experienced Kaizen practitioner and a qualified executive coach, with many years' hard-won experience driving business efficiency, employee engagement and business growth strategies.

On strategy, Marion is very clear: 'There's a big gap many businesses face when driving purpose – it's called executional failure. Many of Africa's best companies have developed great strategies and some practice Kaizen and use other continuous improvement tools. But what is important is locking all the elements together into a system that can be practiced daily and consistently by every last person on the shop floor. Then the strategy becomes fully embedded in the business; managed by a process and not by functions.'

Chapter 3

Seeking Insights

If you accept that Marketing is the science of persuasion, then you cannot ignore the contribution of the test tube labelled 'Market Research'. How can you persuade someone to try something new, if you don't understand why they do what they do? Human beings are complex beings: their motivations and values are not always self-evident. Businesses that make unsupported assumptions about consumer behaviour usually fail to achieve commercial success.

Professional Marketers have a solution for this. They make themselves experts on current and likely consumer behaviour by searching for insights to inform their campaign development. They aim to become so well-informed that they can stand in front of more senior colleagues and convince them to adopt a course of action.

Less professional Marketers don't display this drive. They regard Market Research as an optional extra, and often bend it to justify their actions. This expediency undermines the credibility of their profession. So, in this chapter we'll explore the value of insights and explain why you simply cannot market without them.

Insights – what are they?

In Africa, we rightly place a high value on education, but sometimes we are drawn to appearance rather than substance. We follow fashions in language. Our 'proper' use of English is still quite dated and formal. How often have you been in a meeting to explore modalities? I have been in plenty and yet before I came to Africa I had never grappled with a modality. It's a hangover from colonial civil service days.

Later came NGO-speak. The Aid Sector's almost impenetrable argot, laced with hidden meaning. Capacity building (but not so fast that we do ourselves out of another year's contract). Sustainability (deciding which local staffers will get the laptops after we leave) and so on. Now the professional classes have discovered Marketing-speak. Not just Marketers, for whom this is essential armour, but others too. Financial Managers who want to appear current. Sales Directors who need to survive corporate evolution.

As with all 'closed' languages, it's important to use new words to describe new situations, but avoid valueless redefinition of what is already understood. And it is vital to be clear what these new words really mean. 'Insight' is one such word. Not really new. In fact, long understood to be connected with perception. But, when coupled with words like consumer or category, it must be learned anew. An insight is the basic foundation of sound Marketing. I like to define an insight as an actionable piece of intelligence.

Good Marketers and better business people are naturally perceptive, so they look for insights unconsciously. Being fat and forty makes many women unhappy, so that is a consumer insight. Being at boarding school makes some children homesick, so is that. When you apply insights to business, you can identify opportunities. Homesickness at school might lead to 'back to school' promotion opportunities for brands that are familiar from home.

A good test of an insight is to ask: 'so what?'. Many snippets of information are not insights because they are not actionable. The 'so what?' challenge helps you to decide whether they are actionable or simply interesting.

Industries that are not very good at Marketing often get stuck on one insight for too long. Some mobile phone companies are still stuck on the original insight that people seek the empowerment that personal communications delivers. That's no longer relevant in markets with several mobile networks. Instead, they should be working to identify the next insight to power their brand's appeal. Not resting idly on a category benefit.

If you get this process wrong, you may create products or build services and then have to look around for a market to sell them to. That can be disastrous; lack of insight can create problems on a huge scale. In 1928 the motor tycoon Henry Ford bought up vast tracts of land in Brazil. His plan was to axe the rainforest and plant enough rubber trees to tyre all the cars he was going to make. Henry didn't leave it there. Around the plantation he attempted to create a model American town for his workers. With paved roads, shingled houses, picket fences, lawns and even a golf course.

But his vision lacked two important insights he might have discovered had he been less self-assured. First, the rainforest of Brazil is home to a monster caterpillar fond of eating trees, for whom the rubber plant was a novel and delicious dish. Secondly, the rural people of Brazil had no pressing need for shingle roofs or nine irons. What they really wanted at the end of a long day in the forest were bars, brothels and the excitement of the occasional knife fight. Within five years Fordlandia* was a wasteland, and the utopian community of Ford's dreams a sweltering disease-ridden hellhole.

So, how should you go about finding a consumer insight? Engage a reputable Market Research company on a small test project among customers and prospects. And when they come to present their findings, be prepared to ask "So what?".

*Read 'Fordlandia' by Greg Grandin (Icon Books) to find out more about a disaster created by ignorant hubris.

First published September 2012

What is Consumer Confidence?

In the USA, the University of Michigan publishes a monthly consumer confidence index. According to the BBC Business website 'every blip and dip of the University of Michigan's monthly consumer survey is chewed over obsessively by market pundits.' Here in Africa we don't get this sort of information on a regular basis. When it comes, it's worth a quick read. And Marketers who do so should ponder whether or not to adjust their forecasts.

Consumer confidence is the degree of optimism consumers feel about the overall state of the national economy and their personal financial situation within it. Having recently read a number of these surveys, it is clear to me that the latter strongly influences the former. Particularly in markets where the general public are neither well-informed about macro-economic trends nor the realities of business performance.

Africa is a large and diverse continent. We have to keep saying that for the benefit of those folks who still think we're a country. And, in such a huge place, there are bound to be very significant differences in consumer attitude. Right now, in Ivory Coast, people are less concerned about economics than they are about being hit on the head by a French missile.

Several African governments are looking forward to the perceived blessings of becoming an oil producer. But, as yet, the likely benefits of the black harvest are not clearly understood by consumers. The Modern Ghana News has just reported that local consumer confidence dipped in January 2011, and attributed it mainly to a 30% rise in fuel prices. That sends a confusing signal to people living on the shore of an oil lake, doesn't it?

Meanwhile the Bank of Ghana Composite Index of Economic activity was up 10.5% in 2010, citing improvements in revenues from tourism, social security contributions, manufacturing, ports and harbours. Clearly, the macro-economic message isn't getting through to ordinary people. And the reaction of the Governor of the Central Bank of Ghana was to say: 'there's no cause for alarm'. I think I first heard those words spoken in the movie 'Towering Inferno', and more recently during a Japanese nuclear accident.

In South Africa, consumer confidence also dipped in the fourth quarter of 2010. It measured 14 on the Bureau for Economic Research index but, in fairness, the high in 2010 was 15 and that was a huge improvement on 2009 when the index averaged 2 points. Back in June 2008, South African consumer confidence was minus 6 on the same scale. So perhaps the biggest learning from this is that the confidence curve in South Africa is something of a roller coaster ride.

Turning to Kenya, global research giant TNS has just released the fifth wave in a programme of consumer confidence measurement. The sample was nationally representative of adults over 18 years of age. And it reveals that Kenyan consumer confidence has reduced dramatically. Overall confidence in the economy of the country is down 18%. This is statistically significant. 93% of respondents disagree with the statement 'Jobs are easy to find.' And only 23% agree with the statement 'Jobs will be easier to find in the next 6 months.'

Six months ago, 52% thought business conditions would improve, now that number has dropped to 35%. Marketers should note that only 45% of Kenyans think their household income will increase in the next six months, down from 62% last September. Brand Managers will have to work harder to align their offers with the prevailing attitude of consumer caution.

Interestingly, this pessimism doesn't seem to be shared by Nairobi's business community. Recent CEO-level meetings have been briefed on growth in Sub-Saharan Africa driven by a favourable external environment, ongoing structural reform, booming demographics, strong commodity prices and consumer goods sales. South Africa and the BRIC countries are seen as being active participants in this trend.

So, once again, the man and woman in the street may not be receiving the right macro-economic messages. If this continues, consumer spending will nosedive. So, in amongst the reporting of the Ocampo Six and sundry other political complexities, Kenyans would really benefit from hearing some good news on the economic front.

That said, you can have too many statistics. Here's a favourite story of mine, in which a statistician was participating in a scientific experiment. His head was placed inside a lit oven, and his feet inside a cold freezer. Interviewed afterwards, he commented that: 'on balance, the temperature had been quite comfortable'.

First published April 2011

Insights on brand equity

Hindsight is a wonderful thing. In Marketing, it's the last thing we need but too often it's what our Market Research reports give us. That's really not the fault of the researchers. As we'll discuss below, the best of them are future-focused and constantly innovating new approaches. It's more the fault of the people who buy research: for acting habitually, and not pausing to think before they commission a project.

True, Market Research performs an important role in understanding present reality. But that isn't the be-all and end-all. How often have I read customer surveys put together in a rush by a Marketing Manager? With little or no budget, and insufficient time for thorough fieldwork. And polling the kind of questions you'd use if you were selecting a primate for the Space Programme. The results of such surveys are generally used in one of two ways. Defensively – to protect the idle. Or offensively – to put the finger on another department. So, on the whole, it's no wonder that customer surveys are universally loathed inside companies.

Market Research can give you a useful benchmark, but only if you are planning to do something about it. If you are, the questions you ask should probe areas of possible future activity. You may also be interested in assessing the impact of technology; the real benefit of a larger branch network; the most relevant behaviours to train into your customer-facing staff. You may wish to make your branding clearer and more appealing. If so, the research should aim to give you something more helpful than hindsight: and that is foresight.

You see, customers and prospects are not bogged down by your present reality. They touch your brand, then go on to touch a dozen more before bedtime. They alight on the petals of your business like a butterfly. When times are bad, they may not even notice you. When times are good, they may take your brand for granted. Far too many of us fixate on cause and effect when interpreting consumer behaviour. But that's not how consumers think or feel.

So, what can a good research company do to improve your Marketing foresight? Rosie Hawkins, Global Head of Brand Communication at TNS tells us: 'Brand equity scores reveal how consumers feel about a brand. The only glitch up to now is the process has taken too long. This means you need to look at predictive brand equity scores.' When Rosie talks about predictive brand equity, she means assessing the future relevance and appeal of a brand to its chosen publics. To do this, modern Research Companies are harnessing the immediacy and power of the Internet. They scrape Twitter, Google+, Facebook, LinkedIn and other social networks and combine that with searches on Google, Yahoo and Bing. They also consider content from relevant blogs: for example, salon blogs for hair care products. Rosie says, 'We crunch the data to provide an easy-to-understand brand equity score, and rich and early insights to explain what is happening.'

Nowadays, researchers are finding that they have to use an extra level of interpretation when they delve into social media. The use of language there is very different, and presents new challenges like filtering out bias in blog commentaries. This is necessary, because everyone who has a following must also have an angle.

Using the Internet for research is cheap, without producing the redundant information I always come across when clients tell me they did their customer satisfaction survey in-house. It takes some hard thinking to come up with the right questions, but the mental effort is worthwhile. All the companies I advise now use the Internet for research as much as for brand engagement. Rosie Hawkins is bullish about predictive brand equity studies. 'They usher in a new era in which Marketers spend their time looking at prospective opportunities and pre-empting risks, not looking over their shoulders at past events that they are powerless to influence.'

First published June 2015

The Order Effect

As African markets become more consumer-driven, business leaders are obliged to master more of the skills needed to improve brand success. In particular, business owners in relatively young entrepreneurial businesses, who haven't yet developed a professional Marketing resource.

One of the prerequisites for business success is access to Market Research. You simply cannot direct the actions of a brand without understanding the consumer context. It's like flying an aircraft at night with no terrain avoidance radar.

One of the challenges facing professional Market Researchers is how to avoid skewed or biased results. And it may interest you to know that the order in which questions are asked has a bearing on this. Try reading this list of words quickly: Pen, carton, shell, butter, spanner, apple, wrapper, zebra.

Now cover the list with your hand, and see how many you can remember. Most people remember the first one (pen) and the last one (zebra), but not so many in between.

How do we know that? Because we understand that the order of the list changes how you think and respond. The same thing happens when you give respondents a list of answer choices. The first and the last answer stick out, and the middle tends to get ignored. For example:

Question 3. What is the best young adult literary series of the last ten years?

- *The Harry Potter series*
- *The Hunger Games series*
- *The Twilight series*
- *The Percy Jackson series*

In this list, more respondents will pick Harry Potter and Percy Jackson simply because they are the first and last choices. In survey language, that's called the Response Choice Order Effect. And the reason why people often pick the first answer option is because of a behaviour known as 'satisficing'. Respondents start with the first option, thinking about all the reasons why Harry Potter might or might not be the best series of the last ten years. They then do the same thing for the other options on the list. As respondents go down the list, they start getting a bit tired. So, they begin to satisfice. They stop paying close attention and skim over the last options in the list. This leaves the top choices in the list with a much stronger case than the bottom ones.

The term satisfice was given its current meaning by Herbert Simon in 1956; combining 'satisfy' and 'sacrifice'. So the satisficing solution satisfies some criteria and sacrifices others. Studies of voting in elections have also shown that the order of candidates' names on a ballot affects vote totals. This is one reason why ballots should always randomise the order of candidates' names. In the 2000 US Presidential Election, George W. Bush got 9 percent more votes when he was listed first on the ballot paper than when he was listed last!

And why might people pick the final response? Well, satisficing comes in here too. Again, respondents do the hard thinking work for the first few options, then get tired and begin to satisfice. When they stop thinking critically about the last few choices it can actually make them seem more appealing. This is compounded by an effect called recency, which occurs when the last thing you heard sticks in your mind.

If you are keen on conducting your own surveys, you can counteract these effects the same way that professional research companies do. You have to randomise the options, so that each person sees the list in a different order. If you have an order list or a rating scale, you can flip the options, so some of your respondents see a list that begins with Harry Potter and ends with Percy Jackson, and others see a list that begins and ends vice versa.

Flipping the options means that any order effects will balance themselves out, and your data quality will be enhanced. For a great way to get started with your own simple surveys, go to the free online survey tool **www.surveymonkey.com** and have an inquisitive dabble.

First published October 2013

Privacy and research

I'm an Apple fan. I'm not too sure how well Apple is sticking to its original brand promise to the market, but I'm still prepared to give it some leeway. I like the system and I love the aesthetics of its products. I may even buy the IPhone 6, even though I admit to the growing appeal of the Samsung range.

While tinkering idly on my IPhone the other day, I received an unsolicited message from Facebook. It was very friendly and non-threatening. The message told me that Facebook was moving on and if I wanted to access Facebook messages on my phone, I had to join them on a new App called Facebook Messenger. To encourage me, Facebook also told me how many of my friends have moved.

To be honest I would have downloaded the App instantly and, along with everyone else, I would have ignored the terms and conditions attached. Wasn't it Apple who once produced spoof T&C's that permitted the brand to sell your soul to the Devil – just to prove that no one reads the small print? But I became distracted, and didn't make the download.

Perhaps that was fortuitous for, since then, I have become aware of growing concerns about what Messenger enables Facebook to do. If you read the Terms and Conditions of Facebook Messenger and then sign them, you are authorising the brand to do a number of things that threaten your personal privacy. For example, it can delete, edit or send SMS messages on your phone. It can do similar things inside your address book; including adding new contacts you may not know. More disturbingly, it can take photographs and video footage of you, using both the front screen and back camera on your device. Even when you think the phone is on standby i.e when the screen itself appears black.

This comes on a day when the international media is full of the news that several celebrities have had 'selfies' – intimate photographs and video footage – hacked from their smartphones and sold on the Internet for $100 per view. Jennifer Lawrence, star of the Hunger Games, is one such victim. So is Mary Winstead, a horror film star who subsequently tweeted: 'To those of you looking at photos I took with my husband years ago in the privacy of our home, I hope you feel great about yourselves. Knowing those photos were deleted long ago, I can only imagine the creepy effort that went into this.'

Social media geeks tell me that these hidden permissions are designed to help Apple research customer information. If Facebook knows what you are talking about or looking at, it is better placed to direct relevant advertising your way. If this is the case then these activities now fall under the broad heading of Market Research. In the world of professional Market Research, companies and industry bodies are careful to publish guidelines on how the information they collect may be retained and used. I wonder, does such discipline apply to Facebook?

The commotion over Facebook Messenger's Terms of Service highlights a couple of important issues with the apps that many of us use these days. One is that free products are not truly free: someone has to pay for their development, deployment, and maintenance. So that funding is commonly sourced by serving up paid-for ads to the users. Naturally, advertisers want to be able target and personalise their ads to specific groups of viewers. That targeting requires knowledge about users' geographic locations, ages, browsing habits and so on.

Let's be aware that this is the trade-off we unwittingly accept as payment for free apps. And let's be careful what pictures and other content we create on our devices.

First published September 2014

Here are 5 tips to help you discover priceless insights

▶ Insights Tip 1 – understand human needs

You'd think it a truism that all great brands address a fundamental human need. But many brands in Africa were created to satisfy other publics: company shareholders' being prominent among them. That helps to explains why very few African brands ever appear on global rankings, because they rarely address a fundamental human need.

Some human needs are of a low order, like safety, nourishment and cleanliness. But, as society develops, higher order needs like recognition, altruism and self-actualisation come into play. That time has now arrived in Africa.

Colgate, the world's most successful toothpaste brand, built its foundation upon the understanding that the human need for fresh breath in social situations was far more important than taking satisfaction in clean teeth. So, while every other toothpaste product was banging on about clean choppers, the Colgate brand promised confidence. And what worked in 1960's America and Europe worked just as well when the brand came to Africa in the 1980's. As we Marketers moved toothpaste into smaller tubes and pushed distribution down to the smallest kiosk we found that new users began with a vigorous brushing just once a week. On Sunday morning – to give them greater social confidence in church. In fact, the claim 'Fresh Breath Confidence' worked better than more modern Western promises about cavities because African people naturally enjoy strong, healthy teeth.

Johnnie Walker Whisky doesn't enjoin you to 'Keep on walking' because it values personal fitness. The clever people at Diageo understand that, for most folk, personal achievement palls without the opportunity for public recognition. So, Diageo uses the brand to help us to imagine a successful life journey and provides us with branded beacons to light our way. The first beacon is Johnnie Walker Red, a workmanlike blended whisky with just enough Islay malt to make it quirky and a pack design which connotes a value higher than the price paid. 'Drink Red Label,' says Johnnie Walker, 'and you are taking your first step on the road to success.'

Further along that road lie more enticing beacons and the opportunity for more conspicuous consumption. It's not enough to enjoy a Walker Black or Double Black or Gold ... you must be seen to drink it. Walk beyond that point and you are expected to demonstrate some discernment. It's not enough to have the money for a glass of Johnny Walker Blue or Green. You need to be able to tell the story of the brand variant and describe the taste profile in language mined from a richer adjectival trove. Here we have recognition giving way to the desire for self-actualisation.

Brands that don't link their promise to a fundamental human need almost always struggle to succeed. Their promise just isn't compelling enough. Some brands try to suggest that popularity has a value, but 'Mombasa's Favourite Flip-Flip' is as likely to evoke dissent in that coastal city as scorn further inland. Other brands lean towards ludicrous over-claim. Yet batteries that claim to be 'Simply the best' lay themselves wide open to failure when put to the test by consumers.

Some brands that fail to connect with the needs of the consumer may reflect boardroom hubris. The kind of senior level company conversation that puts customers last. This is signalled by a brand promise that is entirely inwardly focused and self-satisfied. For example, the people charged with rebuilding Kenya Airways yet again might do well to drop the slogan 'The Pride of Africa'.

First published May 2017

▶ Insights Tip 2 – walk in your customers' shoes

Successful businesses are built on superior senses. Senses of timing, opportunity, responsibility and even humour. But none of these is as important as the ability to sense the market.

Bill Gates, Sam Walton and Richard Branson all brought this sense to the businesses they founded. Here in Africa, large enterprises are growing and spreading beyond their domestic markets driven by leaders with just such senses. Who would have thought that the biggest retail bank by branch footprint would have originated in Togo? It's called Ecobank.

Paying attention to customers is not a new idea, but very often CEOs see this as the responsibility of the Sales or Marketing Departments. They themselves can become distracted by discussions with international partners, banks, private equity funds, government officials, and chest-thumping industry sessions with their competitors. The more this happens, the more their own intelligence about the market becomes second- or even third-hand. And it's hard to apply superior senses to third-hand information.

This is compounded by senior managers confusing information with knowledge. Even if you have information from all levels of the distribution channel, you won't necessarily see how each customer relates to the next. Or how they see you against your competitors.

Some years ago, I worked with a global petroleum company. Every quarter, they diligently assembled their leadership team to listen to a Market Research presentation. This was a very long meeting, as the downstream business of the company was large and complex. It was made longer by a very verbose presenter who took us down the hill, around the houses and back up the hill again. Like many researchers in Africa at the time, he was unable to suggest concrete points of action beyond the very obvious. Example: customers say you are expensive, so lower your prices.

A bigger surprise was that the company's leadership group wasn't action-focused. To be honest, they were more concerned with how their overseas superiors saw them. And as that depended on them executing global initiatives to a predetermined template, they showed little interest in the local customer information being presented to them. I attended six of these meetings, and it became the Marketing equivalent of Groundhog Day. Their CEO never attended.

Since then, I've become a fan of customer personification. This involves the senior team taking the time and trouble to profile customers from a wide range of information sources. Face-to face-interviews and salesforce reports married to general information about society gleaned from the Internet, media and word-of-mouth. This helps to builds a qualitative picture rather than a quantitative one. And it is qualitative information that CEOs and their Marketing teams need if they are to develop the superior senses we are talking about.

Customer profiling can be a fun, team-based activity. Making up large boards populated with photographs of typical customers in their living and working environments. Noting their hopes, and fears. Plotting where your own brand might fit into their lives. Involving your Advertising Agency in the process adds more colour to the picture because they have experience of many market segments. Learning how consumers see chicken products might actually inform the way you position your dairy brand.

Customer profiling is not a precise exercise. You can pull it apart if you are so minded. But, bringing a picture of the target consumer to your leadership meetings reminds everyone, from CFO to Production Director, that your business exists to serve human beings. When you remember that, you can apply your superior senses to addressing their present and future needs.

First published April 2014

▶ Insights Tip 3 – sort the wood from the trees

By now you'll have gathered I'm a fan of Market Research. I don't understand how anyone in a market-driven economy would think of conducting business without it. But I'm also a critic of poorly conducted, templated studies conducted by research companies who are short on cash or ethics, or both. Those businesses with quasi-professional names, and Powerpoint templates with 'insert client name here'.

Fortunately, nowadays in Africa we have professional Market Research associations that combine the best of global and local practises. But their higher standards tend to make tariffs pricey, and African business still has low tolerance for the cost of research. All too often, we ditch a study or postpone it. Worse still, we commission research but pressure the provider to screw down his costs. In my experience, screwing down research costs screws up the delivery.

Scrimping on research is not a solely African problem. Many international companies who come to do business here are surprisingly lax when considering research in their Marketing mix. For a fraction of the amount of money they spend with lawyers and bankers (and on hiring spurious local expertise) they could start their business with a research reality check. Validating whether a business idea that works so brilliantly in Belgium will press consumer buttons in Africa.

I'm increasingly involved in advising Foreign Direct Investors, and every new project provides me with fresh insights. Some of these can prevent the kind costly and public failure that we've seen in telecoms (Orange) and beer (Castle Lager), where a foreign brand thinks it is sufficient to say 'we're famous, and now we're here'.

Other insights can dramatically improve adoption rates. If you discover that consumers are happy to access your brand via SMS, but website is a step too far, you can reduce your investment in digital even though your HQ in Baltimore mandates it.

How people in Africa react to brand names, indeed how they pronounce them, can also be quite unexpected. And tastes change very quickly. Twenty years ago, many brand or business names began with Ken, or Zam, or Tan or Ug. Ten years ago, we had a riot of nomenclature related to mobile telephony. M- this and M- that. More recently we've had a lot of E- and I- based names. And I've discovered that African consumers are very open to fresh ideas for brand names. In a recent project, a name that was completely abstract outperformed all other options. Even though it was deliberately made-up, respondents felt it implied a friendly, family-based business. If we hadn't used Market Research, we'd never have found that out.

How people react to logo colours and designs delivers even greater understanding. In focus group discussions, colours that reflect that category norm – like blue and green for banks – are initially warmly received because they are familiar. But when they are shown other colour options, respondents quickly tell you that they are bored with blue and green. And that can open a wider conversation about being bored with bank services!

The lesson for modern business is this. Always push for the best possible consumer insights to help you sort the wood from the trees.

First published November 2015

▶ Insights Tip 4 – handle research data with care

Time spent in reconnaissance is seldom wasted. So say the textbooks, paraphrasing the ancient oriental strategist Sun Tsu. As a former reconnaissance soldier, I have some issues with this. I spent 15 years looking for the Russians, but they never came.

Nonetheless, the thought that any commercial decision can be taken 'based on the numbers' or on 'what the sales force tells us' or 'what my investment club thinks' does ring alarm bells for me. For the simple reason that it completely ignores the role of the consumer in influencing business success.

Businesses that ignore the consumer do not build lasting brands. But, as I travel around Africa, it's surprising to learn that business is making less use of Market Research as we move into the second decade of the 21st Century. Companies are entering new markets or categories with the insouciance of the Lagos taxi driver – who launches his passengers into the traffic and only then looks over his shoulder to see what's coming.

There are three reasons for this bad business habit. Firstly, successive recessions in Africa have pushed Marketing investment down, and Market Research seems difficult to justify to a hatchet man from global headquarters. Secondly, fast-growing African businesses are in arrogant denial about opinions that do not coincide with those of the big boss. There are some very big bosses now, in banking, airlines and telecoms. Their personal brands sometimes dwarf those of their companies, and no big boss wishes to be gainsaid. But, for the good of the shareholders, perhaps they should be.

Thirdly, I really don't think that the research industry in Africa has helped itself. Value-for-money perceptions of research have been damaged by the revelation that some companies do not carry out proper fieldwork. instead pocketing fat cheques for fielding ghost workers. Then rather too many Market Researchers equate volume with value, producing huge reports that are endlessly discursive. I suspect they picked up this habit from the NGO Sector, which loves any debate that prolongs their project until the next funding round.

But let's stay positive. Good Market Research can indeed intimate likely consumer behaviour. It can test brand positioning options. Most important of all, it can objectively measure performance. Something that is definitely in the best interest of the shareholders.

Let me end with news of the silliest Market Research project of recent years, announced in global news media last week. The Kenya Government is tendering for a research company to assess the number of gay people in the country's population. As homosexuality is a criminal offence carrying a sentence of up to 18 years, I suspect that respondents will be somewhat shy.

So, anyone of an entrepreneurial bent should tender for this project immediately. Secure in the knowledge that no expectation of results means no requirement to provide a real service. It will be money for old rope!

First published October 2012

▶ Insights Tip 5 – talk to a woman

Book launches are always exciting. Particularly when someone you know and respect has committed themselves to print. I am eagerly awaiting the publication of 'Authentic African Leadership' by my friend Gail Cameron. The book is a compilation of true stories of leadership from corporate and institutional life in South Africa. Gail's role as a top executive coach has given her access to some extraordinary figures in that country's public life. And it's a pleasant surprise to see how many of them are women.

The business guru Tom Peters, writing on human talent in his Essentials Collection, emphasised the importance of accelerating women into leadership positions. He says that for too long we have recognised women's rights but ignored their strengths. And I wholeheartedly agree.

Gail Cameron believes that women's exceptional faculties are particularly well-suited to meet the demands of the 21st century business in Africa and beyond: 'They are talented with words and often better at languages. Women win most international speaking contests.' She suggests that women are also much better than men at reading nonverbal behaviour. They are emotionally sensitive and generally have more empathy than men. And at work, the very best women prefer co-operating to commanding. They readily accept ambiguity, and they honour intuition over rationality.

Today women earn one third of all science doctorates awarded in the world. In the United States, women have outnumbered men in college for more than a decade and now more are receiving more Bachelor's Degrees in scientific fields than men. Gail Cameron says: 'We live in the era of the ascendancy of people-oriented leadership. This is primarily a relational and participatory approach that requires a commitment to listen and understand. These are the strengths of the best women leaders.'

Yet many Marketers and male-dominated leadership teams are ignoring the biggest implication of this. Consider the buying power of women, and not just as consumers. In the US, women own 10.6 million businesses. They employ 19.1 million people. Their revenue exceeds Germany's GDP of 2.4 trillion dollars. And, here in Africa, casual observation alone will reveal that more than half of our small enterprises are run by women.

Thankfully, some enterprises are now beginning to create brands with women in mind. And not just in the personal care category. Again, in the States, Dutch Boy Paint has shown how a simple, women-friendly design changes can improve sales. Their paint container is easier to carry and easier to store: it makes house painting a lot less messy and arduous for women.

Mattel, the toy manufacturer, is now creating building blocks for little girls that include plastic squares, balls, triangles, squiggles, flowers and sticks in pastel colours with rounded corners. This is a deliberate evolution from the linear play patterns and angular materials it makes for boys.

In Africa, Marketers have long kept the housewife in a box. They imagine her primary role is to be the purchaser of Fast Moving Consumer Goods for extended families. But we should give credit to the financial services sector as the first to recognise women in groups and as individuals – as target markets for tailored products. Nowadays we're beginning to see female-centric communication for life insurance and mortgage products. A hopeful sign that women are being considered more seriously as a target audience.

Perhaps it's now time to commission some insightful research to work out how your brand might appeal more authentically to women?

First published November 2010

Let's meet an
Investigator of Insights

Ndirangu wa Maina

Ndirangu wa Maina is the Managing Director of Consumer Insight Africa, which owns the Market Research business Consumer Insight, the trade Marketing firm Gap Marketing and VoicesAfrica, one of the largest online research panels in Africa. He founded the group in 1998.

Before that he was an adman at Saatchi & Saatchi and later McCann Erickson, where he was the Deputy Managing Director for Kenya and Strategic Planning Director for Africa. Consumer Insight is now a leading African Market Research business, conducting studies in over 30 countries on the continent. The company specialises in understanding the drivers of consumer behaviour. Over the years Ndirangu has created a portfolio of proprietary branded studies, including Dama on the socio-economic impact of women; Digitalk on consumption of digital media; Holla on youth lifestyles and trends, and Wakenya on the changing psyche of Kenyans.

He is a recipient of both Marketing Society of Kenya Warrior and H.K. McCann Leadership Awards. He has served on the Marketing Society of Kenya Council, the Kenya College of Accountancy Board and HIV-Free Generation Board.

Speaking about Market Research, Ndirangu says: 'As human beings we are always researching, whether we know it or not. Good researchers listen to what people mean, not what they say. They remember that what people don't say is often as important as what they do say. They also know that consumers are great at identifying needs, but not so hot at proposing innovations.'

Chapter 4

Target Identification

To be effective, Marketers must always decide to whom they are Marketing. They must choose to address certain types of people, and ignore others. The less selective they are, the more money they will need to spend to reach a wider audience. And the creation of relevant messaging becomes almost impossible.

As human beings, we spend our lives engaging with other people. Understanding who fits where, and who likes whom. In his extraordinary book 'Sapiens: A brief history of humankind' Yuval Noah Harari advances the theory that our species became dominant on the planet partly thanks to its ability to exchange a stream of rich information about individuals within the group. This gossip enabled Homo Sapiens to form a picture of who could be relied upon, and for what. Who could be trusted, and who might betray, when a truly collaborative effort was required.

Competent Marketers extend the use of this skill to cover entire populations. They make a point of classifying the people who might buy their brand in a variety of different ways. The most basic of which is, of course buying power, indicated by socio-demographic status. In the early years of Marketing in Africa we all used the socio-demographic model developed to classify European households. Based on the occupation and income of the head of the family, this divided any population into a series of segments from A to E. It was a start, because before then any African population had been regarded as broadly homogenous. And it helped in one important way. By defining the readership, listenership and later viewership of mass media channels, socio-demographics made the process of channel selection and advertising investment a little more objective.

Much later, in the 1990's, the South Africans came up with a more complex segmentation, based on their observation of housing types and the household contents within. Known as the LSM or Living Standard Measures this didn't add much to existing thinking in Africa. It really was a product of a society that habitually discriminated against people, rather than one that sought *to understand and include. In the rest of Africa, it caused some confusion and broad dissatisfaction as puzzled Marketers tried to bend the model to fit much less rigid societies.*

The problem with both models was that they failed to consider people as human beings. To probe their motivations and values in life. To understand why certain types of people practice particular habits. Why individuals participate in consumer categories that their socio-economic status would, on the face of it, prevent them from so doing.

Fortunately, good work on this new kind of segmentation was already underway in other global markets. By the late 1980's Marketers were able to identify target audiences more meaningfully through this study of Psychographics. The groundwork for this was actually laid by Abraham Maslow in his 1943 paper 'A theory of Human Motivation'.

*Today this range of psychographic segmentation options continues to proliferate, with major consumer goods companies often creating their own category-specific models. Most international advertising agencies created their own as well. Having worked in three global communications groups, I tend to favour the Young & Rubicam Cross-Cultural Consumer Characterisation Model **www.issuu.com/youngandrubicam/docs/4cs** for its simplicity and clear illustration of behavioural differences. In this chapter, we look at the benefits of targeting specific audiences.*

Start with emotion

Whenever the subject of targeting surfaces in modern Marketing discussions in Marketing parlance, the word 'segmentation' inevitably comes up as well. Marketers usually begin by talking about their potential customers according to the socio-economic segment they're in.

We'll be looking at different consumer segments throughout this chapter. But, before we get into those, let's look at an approach that should be applied across them all. That's the need to understand each target's emotional make-up. Considering consumers as human beings, and not just as numbers.

I often find that Marketers approach Africa as a lumpen mass. They see a huge continent of similarly disadvantaged people. Not just disadvantaged economically; but stripped of much of their humanity, too. Consequently, many Marketing meetings rubbish good ideas for communication and engagement because they dare to address the target consumer as a human being. Give me a nod if you've heard these kind of comments:

'We can't use humour, it's too subjective' or 'The Bottom of the Pyramid won't understand this' and, very often, 'That's too aspirational for rural people.'

You might think these put-downs come from international Marketers with little empathy for the African consumer. But, by and large, they don't. Instead they come from indigenous African Marketers.

If truth be told, international Marketers in Africa have come a long way in the last twenty years. In my early advertising days, we used to have Vice President Bob fly in from Tampa, Florida and order us to televise 'that great spot from Peru. Just dub it into your local language'. Nowadays the Vice President is likely to be called Maina or Sarpong, and have a blend of local market experience and international exposure. So, thankfully, we rarely see dubbed advertising featuring Scandinavian mountains, cartoon beavers, or Honduran housewives with dodgy lip synch nowadays. In some ways, I miss them.

By contrast African Marketers often distance themselves from genuine opportunities to engage fellow African consumers. They tend to look down on the consuming public from their shiny corporate offices. So, it's no surprise that African Marketers rarely produce advertising that goes beyond templated ideas. It's dull, conventional stuff we see on our TV screens every night. Plump, comfortable-looking African people holding a product and smiling beatifically. Once I even saw a TV spot for cement that tried to construct a very tenuous link between concrete and the happiest moments of family life. This kind of work is safe and largely ineffective.

Fear is an emotion that was used in early public health and social Marketing campaigns. Nowadays, received wisdom tells us that fear is counter-productive. But I don't agree. If you ever look at international campaigns for road safety, domestic fire prevention or similar hazards, the most effective ones dramatise the horrific consequences of misadventure. They force the viewer to face up to reality, and that is very impactful.

But the emotion that is most roundly ignored in African advertising is envy. In fact, if you mention envy as a consumer motivation most Marketers will purse their lips. It's not seemly or respectable to admit that envy exists in our societies. But is it wrong for people to desire something they don't have? National liberation campaigns always used a good helping of envy in their messaging. Generations of social improvement has been fuelled by the 'have-nots' wanting what the 'haves' have. Education. Better housing. Freedom of communication. A double latte with vanilla syrup.

Surely African consumers have the propensity to be as envious as anyone else?

In America, they have been measuring happiness for decades. In 1936, 32% of Yanks claimed to be very happy but that percentage hasn't risen since. Despite eighty subsequent years of progress. A tripling of household incomes; pre-sliced bread; deodorant; colour TV; mobile phones and airline loyalty programmes. None of this has made the average American any happier. But what does make him happier is the knowledge that his standard of living is envied by his neighbours.

I don't believe our burgeoning African middle class is any different. And recent research studies in Africa have even thrown up clear evidence of envy at the Bottom of the Pyramid. BOP consumers value brands just as much as anyone else. Indeed, when money is tight, they rely on brands to reassure them that they are spending wisely. They see more upmarket consumers using brands like Nokia and they want one. Brand association uplifts their spirits and reassures them the product will work for them too. This is a new and fundamental redefinition of value for money. It goes way beyond the 'affordability' which businesses love to signal, but consumers interpret as 'cheap'.

Taboo though it may be, ask yourself whether your brand makes people envious of your customers.

First published August 2010

Appeal to humanity

Over the past two centuries, millions of pieces of advertising have been created all over this world. If you examine them, you will find that many of them conform to a limited range of themes – each with its own predictable styles and motifs.

The reason for this does not lie in the inability of advertisers to create fresh ideas. Instead these themes have emerged to address common points of connection with the consumer. And you find that the best advertising always appeals to a universal human value.

The theme that springs to mind first is the status advertisement. The glamorous appeal to the universal human need to be noticed and admired. Brands that address this need try to make the consumer feel special. They might lend you the charisma you lack or otherwise render you more desirable. Fashion, cosmetics and accessories brands tread this proven path.

Another theme influences those people who sit at the very centre of most societies. Over the years we have given them many names: the Bourgeoisie, the Middle Majority or Middle Class. They're an important audience for any Marketer, and they've never been bigger in Africa than they are today. They are able to give a brand a large and loyal customer base – but only if you win their confidence. By their very nature, these people are averse to new ideas. The theme that appeals to them is security; the celebration of the status quo.

The African Development Bank Group has just published a study indicating that Africa's middle class has now risen to 34% of the total population of the continent. Up from around 23% ten years ago, that translates into 313 million people, all building their nests and exhibiting similar, habitual, family-focused behaviours.

Of course, on a continent as diverse as Africa, the size of this group varies widely from market to market. Liberia has the smallest proportion, with only 4% of its total population in this group. Societies with middle classes forming 30% to 60% of the population include Angola, Ghana and Kenya. The countries on Africa's Mediterranean littoral are largely middle class, with Tunisia topping the bill at over 80%. Their attitude to sudden change makes the events of the recent 'Arab Summer' all the more extraordinary.

In general, this mainstream group will endure iniquity longer than anyone else. Broken political promises, economic hardship, mobile networks that don't work; lacklustre customer service. They just suck it all up.

If you want to connect with these mainstream consumers, you need to address the value they place on security for themselves and for their loved ones. Not just steel bars on the windows, but emotional security and adequate physical comfort. For them, security means avoiding risk. It means belonging to something larger than yourself – an extended family, a home or a congregation. Mainstream adults aspire to the role of responsible mum or dad:

- Being price conscious; watching the pennies and avoiding debt. Making sacrifices and saving for the future, especially for their children's future.
- Blending in; being conformist. Taking comfort from being the same as everyone else.
- Obeying the rules and avoiding confrontation; preserving the status quo. Having a place for everything and everything in its place.

African media is saturated with messaging that addresses this group. Simple, warm emotion is the essential ingredient. People are shown happy, well fed and ... together. Puzzles and ambiguities are avoided, but a good-natured sense of humour is appreciated. Brands that succeed here look familiar and reassuring; they never offend. Often, they maintain continuity with the past.

A mainstream customer base will perpetuate the success of an established brand without too much Marketing effort. But they do make you work hard to launch a new brand. So, the trick is to make it appear safe and established as quickly as you possibly can.

First published July 2011

Shouldn't every brand be a youth brand?

Last year I celebrated my half-century. I know, you can't believe it because I look so young! Anywhere in the world 50 years is a milestone, but here in Africa I am now part of a very small population segment.

A Brand Manager in her thirties is also getting on a bit. She needs to work increasingly hard to remain in touch with younger consumers. But why should she, if her brand is not a 'youth brand'?

Well, the simple answer is that every major brand in Africa should consider how to appeal to young people. That is the existential challenge African brands are going to face, sooner than we think. The average age of all humans on the planet is 28 years. In Italy, it is 43; in Japan 44; in India 26. But in Africa it is under 20.

This age gap has already produced some challenges in the way global brands have been marketed. In very long-lived societies like Sweden, consumer brands may have a target audience ranging from 20 to 60 years of age. Traditionally we would have called that broad group a brand user base rather than a target audience. But contemporary Marketing thinking suggests that if you want your brand to last, you need to segment and address many target audiences simultaneously. With older audiences, the Marketing emphasis has shifted from retention to re-evaluation. Most Swedish consumers know their brand portfolio very well, but can be tempted to reconsider and recommit to brands they have discarded.

In the 1960's, all over the West there was a clear generation gap. Actually, more of a chasm than a gap. Parents who had survived World War Two were austere, responsible, and prepared to sacrifice for the greater good. 1960's teenagers were the opposite: sensualist, experimental, promiscuous and selfish. This gap allowed Marketers to accelerate consumerism by creating brands aligned with the values of the younger generation. Look at any advertising reel from that period: 'The choice of a new generation' became an almost universal brand mantra.

I believe that global brands entering African markets should rediscover the idea of the generation gap because, here and now, it is becoming significant. If we took a family from Africa and drew parallels with Western ones, it would be like giving a modern child a mother from the 1940's and a grandmother from the 1890's. Granny would expect to decide whom the granddaughter will marry. Mum would expect daughter to remain a virgin until she does. But daughter just wants to hang at the coffee shop and play Angry Birds on her Android phone.

In cosmetics, the drive in Africa should be about being pretty for your date, not delaying the effects of ageing. In telephony, Marketers could be offering unexpected levels of styling, and the latest tech trends to spark the interest of young people. Sampling and trial have always been important Marketing techniques. Nowadays they should be used to reassure young people that an established brand is also interested in them. Digital sampling via mobile Internet may well be the best way to put your brand into the hands of young people.

No brand that hopes to succeed in Africa should ignore young people. Indeed, brands that will win here over the next decade will probably target young people first and foremost.

First published February 2011

Stay on top of research trends

Our world doesn't stand still. What worked for Marketers yesterday may not necessarily work tomorrow.

But there's so little investment in consumer research these days that I sometimes think Researchers should sample Marketers to find out what is going on!

Whenever any meaningful research study comes my way, I make it my business to read it. The latest piece, called Wakenya, was recently conducted by Consumer Insight Africa. A similar study on Uganda is planned for 2017. Wakenya sampled 3,500 people aged 13+ from rural and urban areas and across all our counties. It doesn't make seismic revelations, but highlights some trends that are worthy of Marketers' consideration.

Kenyans all cite health and wellbeing as a major concern, but don't act about it in the way you might expect. 42% don't go to the doctor, preferring to self-medicate with home remedies or buy drugs over the counter. Knowing the high incidence of counterfeit drugs and unlicensed pharmacies, I find that worrying. Only 24% trust insurance – and they tend to be older, wealthier urban men. Other Kenyans don't see the value, or simply don't understand the concept, of insurance.

Kenyans continue to marry young: half our ladies marry under 24 years of age. 70% of girls and 50% of boys claim to have been sexually active when they were under 16 years. The only related good news is that young women are increasingly taking responsibility for contraception. The bad news is that young men aren't. Young couples are opting out of formal religious weddings; and the incidence of come-we-stay marriages is on the increase.

Only 41% of Kenyans bank with 'bricks and mortar' institutions. Money is mobile, and over a third of the sample had taken loans from schemes like M-Shwari. Preferred sources of borrowing for men are still friends and family. But relationship saving schemes (Chamas and Saccos) are preferred by women. 1 in 3 Kenyans holds three sim cards – dancing nimbly between them to manage calls, mobile money and data. This will change when the cost of broadband access drops through oversupply.

The big losers in modern Kenya are the traditional media groups, who handled the digital transition badly and are now feeling the pain of eroding relevance. Wakenya reveals that 67% of radio audiences are actually elderly and rural, which presages serious audience decline. Only 22% of Kenyans read newspapers any more. And although television continues to attract younger viewers, they are increasing seeing it free and without commercials – online.

Reviewing the rest of the survey I have a distinct feeling that Kenyans are increasingly doing what they want to do as individuals, not caring whether anyone else thinks that is right or not. That is a major mind-set change.

First published November 2016

Win at the Top of the Pyramid

The African middle class is now expanding. Economists and Marketers like to say that this class is 'emerging', but that doesn't do justice to the millions of Africans who have been building homes, saving for education, going to church and ascending the professional ladder for decades.

Africans who climb higher are often dismissed as a small 'super rich' group. The words 'super rich' are usually used to imply wrong-doing as the source of wealth. Used whenever a journalist wishes to draw our attention to the gap between rich and poor. I've heard it so often that I quite understand why it's called a yawning gap.

But people who do well are not, by default, evil. True, they attract envy. True, they find themselves in positions of great influence. Along the way some falter and lose their moral compass.

Others begin by losing it, then do what they need to do to make money and then try to find it again when their thoughts turn to legacy. But before they have the luxury of legacy, they have to make their way in the world; they have to succeed. Which is why the 'Lions and Lionesses' of Africa should be an important target audience for Marketers here. And like any target audience they can be influenced … but only if you understand what drives them. The core value of successful people is almost always the need for control.

That doesn't sound very nice, but if you stop to think about it, people who are successful usually become so by insisting that things are done their way. Political leaders, business tycoons, military Generals and even the Catholic Church's many Bishops. If you examine their life stories, you will find that taking control was central to their later achievements. Successful people make themselves at home in the Establishment – in the competitive business world, in enduring institutions like churches and clubs. And in these roles their initial contribution is often organisational. They first make a name for themselves by getting things done: chairing a neighbourhood committee; keeping the accounts for a fundraising drive or serving as a school Governor.

Successful people are motivated to meet challenge with achievement. They equip themselves with high levels of personal confidence, firm judgement and great motivational skills. In Africa, more and more women are joining this group. In my view, they will one day lead it. Women here manage the demands of family, career and community with greater success and less agony than their sisters overseas.

So, as a Marketer, how do you succeed with successful people? With your private banking lounges; your top-end safari businesses and your premium spirit brands?

First you have to recognise that an important motivation is separation from the mass. Not only through the prestige your brand offers but in other, subtler ways.

For example, in advertising you should never show them as part of a crowd. You'll notice that Business Class or First Class airline advertising only ever conveys solitary pleasures. Also, as their self-image is one of organising complexity, so the visual style of any advertising should reflect this. Content can be complex, but the presentation must be tidy and ordered. Otherwise they will want to order it, and that is an annoying distraction. Have you noticed how every advertisement for an expensive wristwatch shows the hands at ten to two? Anywhere else would lack balance, and possibly obscure the detail of the face.

Headlines are very important to 'succeeders'. Short and cleverly constructed, they should ideally contain a private joke that is designed to raise a quiet smile. A classic print ad for the The Macallan malt whisky simply shows a bottle of the whisky with a crystal glass holding a generous nip. The background is black, and the bottle is beautifully lit. The copy simply reads, 'For people who sign their own expenses'.

The future may be difficult to control. But successful people are keen to understand the possibilities of a long life. They are determined to preserve themselves and their loved ones with insurance, preventative healthcare and the search for a healthier lifestyle – free from stress.

Which brings me to my final point. The services you render to these people must be impeccable: designed to relieve stress and minimise irritation. If you are in a service industry, you'll already know that a disappointed 'succeeder' can be a roaring lion. But a happy one is just a big old pussycat.

First published February 2013

Here are 5 tips to help you focus on a target audience

▶ Targeting Tip 1 – recognise African men

New behaviours always bring opportunities. And, amongst African men, behaviours are changing fast. For decades, African man has aspired to being a big man, but sometimes ended up disappointingly small. His authority was usually based on tradition; on looking backwards at what has always been. But today, African man is looking forwards and sideways too. His reference points are no longer simple tales from a paternalistic culture featuring male authority figures. His pride is no longer nationalistic – he's keen to belong to the wider world.

As you might expect, these changes are beginning with younger men, but they are not limited to urban dwellers. Social researchers have been telling us for at least a decade that there is little difference between the aspirations of town or countryside. Even if urban Marketers can't help looking down on out-of-towners!

Nowadays some of our banks and more of our financial technology companies are making inroads into serving the previously unbanked. All around us the digital revolution accelerates exponentially every week. Android phones are placing Internet access, and the opportunities that creates, into thousands of new hands every day.

Male role models are changing. Five years ago, most African men would have held their own President in high esteem. In South Africa last week, it was clear that Mr. Zuma is a figure of fun for young professionals. Ask young businessmen from Algiers or Tunis; Harare or Luanda and you are likely to uncover even harsher emotion shown towards national leaders. Instead, soccer players are widely admired. Particularly those bearing the stamp of the

Barclays Premier League. Not just for their skills with the leather, but for their style, internationalism and media-savvy confidence.

Today a Drogba or Essien would pull a crowd bigger than any politician on this continent. Black TV and movie stars come high on the bill too. Idris Elba has appeared in 'The Wire', 'The Office' and now stars in a UK series titled 'Luther'. Adewale Akinnuoye-Agbaje starred in 'Lost', speaks four languages and has a Masters' Degree from the University of London. Fally Ipupa, Congo's inspirational R&B singer, has 33,700 Facebook fans and most of them are men. I wonder whether any of these new role models will grow to be leaders in public life?

Modern African men are spending big money on looking good, and not just on satin shirts and pointy Nigerian shoes. Male grooming products are flying off the shelves. Billboards across the Continent reassure men that international skincare brands are for them. This year Euromonitor forecasts that sales of men's' grooming products will exceed USD 250m in South Africa and USD 17m in Kenya.

Some commentators have dubbed this new male behaviour metrosexualism, but I think we may need to coin our own phrase. Metrosexual goes too far, being defined as a heterosexual male who has a strong aesthetic sense and an inordinate interest in appearance and style, similar to that of homosexual males.

A more interesting word is Afripolitanism. Used to describe African men (and women) who wish to express their identity as a blend of African and International. The urge to travel widely is upon them – not just for knowledge and fashion, but also to assert their confidence as professional people. Smart industries involving technology, creativity and entertainment attract them and provide numerous opportunities to join the Diaspora.

None of this is a surprise to global advertisers, who have observed these trends in other regions for many years. They do however indicate that Africa is truly coming of age as a consumer marketplace. That African men may now be legitimately be grouped with French or Japanese men in global segmentation exercises.

It's a great time to be an African man, and for the brands that address their emerging aspirations.

First published April 2011

▶ Targeting Tip 2 – dignify African women

Here's a fact: women now drive the world economy. They take most of the regular buying decisions for their families and they are discerning consumers in their own right. Harvard Business Review opines that consumer spending by women represents a growth market bigger than China and India combined. Globally, ladies control about $20 trillion in annual consumer spending, and that figure could climb as high as $28 trillion in the next five years. Given those numbers, it would be foolish to ignore or underestimate the female consumer.

And yet many companies do just that. What is the epitome of Marketing to women in Africa? Sanitary protection. Full marks for practicality, and all credit to Procter & Gamble for initially addressing that important need. But, can you name any other Marketing campaigns you have seen that address women effectively? Some banks have had a go at targeting women. But bank Marketers are such sheepish followers that if one launched an account for meerkats, they would all do the same. I wonder how special a generic Womens' Account makes women feel?

For such Marketing to work, a brand will need a Customer Relationship Management (CRM) programme to maintain a regular dialogue with busy women. To find out more about them, and tailor offers at just the right time and price point. It's all about relevance, and relevance takes care, time and commitment from the brand team. Small businesses are often instinctively good at CRM. The local vegetable seller, who slips in an extra maize cob to reward your loyalty. The honey stall that offers you credit. The salon that treats your daughter to free braids, knowing that she has a lifetime of beauty needs ahead of her.

The trouble is, the bigger the business, the harder it is to deliver a personalised service that appears genuine. Recently, Boston Consulting Group fielded a study of how women felt about their work and lives, and how they were being looked after by brands. It turned out there was lots of room for improvement. Learn more about the survey at **www.womenspeakworldwide.com**. Much of what they found would resonate with modern women in Africa. In brief, women feel vastly underserved. They have too many demands on their time and constantly juggle conflicting priorities at work, in the home and within their extended family. Yet few brands have addressed their need for timesaving solutions. Like making it easier to create a healthy meal; giving financial advice without delay; or offering timely opportunities to exercise and stay in shape.

Many newcomers to Africa are astounded to hear that most husbands and wives still keep separate finances and undertake to fulfil separate obligations to the household: 'You do the school fees and I'll pay the utilities'. Nor are those obligations always equitably shared, as many African men reserve the right to change their minds or simply default – just because they can. African women don't have that luxury and, far too often, they end up as single parents. So, brands that keep faith with women, staying relevant through good times and bad, would be especially welcomed. No wonder women's self-help groups and saving clubs have such big bank accounts these days.

Women actually control spending in most categories of consumer goods. Yet many brands still behave as if they had no informed say on purchasing decisions. They continue to offer women poorly-conceived products and services, and outdated Marketing narratives that promote female stereotypes. In a recent painful episode in the US, Dell launched a laptop for women, and made it pink!

The truth is that Marketing to women is no different than Marketing to any other defined target group. It's all about relevance. Female audiences will respond better to psychographic than socio-economic segmentation. It isn't about what she earns or where she lives; it's about her hope and fears and the values she espouses. If you want success in Marketing your brand to women, you should start by really meaning it.

First published September 2014

▶ Targeting Tip 3 – acknowledge youthfulness

How many times have you heard the words, 'We must address the Youth'? In my 25 years in Africa, I must have heard it monthly. From politicians, NGO's and educationalists; even from Marketers!

And, of course, they were right. On a continent of one billion people, 60% of whom have not yet reached majority, the figures are clear enough for the dimmest statistician to grasp. But in Africa average life expectancy is between 40-50 years, so we may need to redefine the descriptor. Is youthfulness an age band or a mind-set?

Youthful people are early adopters; they love to try new things. They pursue careers that were not open to their parents; they adopt new technology. They enter the cash economy earlier, and in larger numbers, than in previous generations. This means that they are becoming consumers in their own right faster than ever before.

We already know lots of facts about young people in Africa, but surprisingly little about their attitudes. And this we must do, for only a mastery of Psychographics (rather than measures of demography or spending power) will turn us into a continent of proficient Youth Marketers.

Let's start with the commonplace name we ascribe to them: the Youth. Whenever I hear that definite article I picture a harassed teenager, in Kumasi or Kibimba, who is the sole and unwitting target of all this attention. 'There he is – the Youth – quickly let us target him!'.

But all young people, like everyone else in the world, are individuals. If you want to align your brand with them, you must understand that individuality is absolutely central to their self-image. This presents Marketers with a problem of focus. If a Brand Manager has difficulty dividing his budget between urban and rural, or between East and West, how on earth is he going to resource individualised Marketing activities? The answer is that he won't be able to, instead he must look for commonalities. And what we have learnt from cross-border Marketing in Africa and the wider world is this. Look for commonality in espoused values before you consider anything else.

Many segmentation models exist to help with this. They talk about Generations X, Y and Z. One of the best I ever encountered called the youth value set 'Explorers'. It's a good name, because it gives a clear indication of likely behaviour. The Explorer segment defines individuality as taking risks and experimenting with life. Leaving the safety of the familiar to find out who you really are. Avoiding obligation; expressing confidence and optimism about the world. Explorers act on impulse and they exhibit a a curious form of materialism – acquiring and discarding possessions rapidly. All of which should fill Marketers with excitement!

Explorers ridicule conventional and stereotyped advertising. In their view, rules must be broken. Communication must be genuinely different. They seek clashing colours; not complimentary shades. Present nothing to them in tables or boxes; resist the urge to dumb things down for them. Instead, set clever puzzles that others can't solve. Make advertising narrowband and starkly relevant. Remember that young people are adept at handling fragmented messages – that's how viral Marketing started.

Explorers are very tribal, but not in the traditional African sense. Instead they form thousands of groups of individuals – each with a real character and identity. Badged with clothing, behaviour and brand associations that mark them out as different. Outside Africa, youth brands are more daring. Brands with attitude; brands that don't compromise. Here in Africa, we don't dare enough, so we don't reap the rich rewards of aligning closely with young people. Not yet, anyway.

First published January 2011.

▶ Targeting Tip 4 – older or wiser?

Africa is all about youth. That said, there are still millions of people on this continent who could be counted as senior citizens in the broadest sense. Our seniors tend to be much younger than those in Western markets: we age sooner and we die earlier. A quick look at any African census confirms this. Malaria, poor sanitation, AIDS, road traffic accidents and resurgent plagues all take their toll on our numbers.

Average life expectancy on the planet is 65 for men and 69 for women. African countries occupy the bottom of the longevity league table. Highest in sub-Saharan Africa is Senegal with an average age of 63. In East Africa, we will live 20% fewer years than the world average. Further South lie countries with the lowest life expectancies: Swaziland, Angola, Botswana, Lesotho, Zimbabwe and South Africa. All suffering from high rates of HIV/AIDS infection that range from 10% to 40% percent of all adults.

I don't think I have ever sat in a Marketing meeting where we have tried to define African senior citizenship – as opposed to downright old age. With the focus on youth, most Marketers use 45 years of age as a pretty absolute cut-off. Beyond that you are considered to be not influence-able at best; in God's waiting room at worst.

And yet, many older African people have survived the early challenges to their disposable income. Kids have grown up, the house or shamba has been built, and business or professional life has matured. It's time for these consumers to spend a little more on themselves. In further education, smarter cars, leisure travel, technology and entertainment. And older consumers are smarter, too. They may appear conservative, but their decision-making skills are at their sharpest. Last weekend I leafed through a study from Canada that suggested getting older really does make you wiser.

It showed that older people use their brains more efficiently than their younger counterparts because they are more likely to shrug off mistakes. Scientists set two groups of participants a task that involved sorting words into pairs, and scanned their brains as they completed them. Challenges included pairing words according to category or initial letter, and picking out words that rhymed. Neuro-imaging scans revealed striking differences between the brains of the older and younger participants when they made a mistake.

In younger people, any error instantly activated several different parts of the brain to help them decide what to do next. However, older people's brains held their fire until the game restarted: only then did they start thinking about what they were going to do. The oldest group (aged 55-75 years) took longer to complete the game but did as well as those aged under 35. Study author Dr. Oury Monchi, of the Institute of Geriatrics at the University of Montreal, compared the results to Aesop's fable of the tortoise and the hare: 'Being able to run fast does not always win the race. You must know how best to use your abilities.'

African seniors will increasingly have money to spend. But they will be a discerning and thoughtful audience, requiring a distinctive Marketing approach that recognises them as a segment in their own right.

First published May 2015

▶ Targeting Tip 5 – help Strugglers escape

Some Marketers make the mistake of viewing the 'bottom' of society as unrewarding. They would rather spend dollars on chubby, shiny-faced middle-income families who need lavatory paper, ice cream, palm oil and beef patties – and not necessarily in that order. They would prefer to encourage you to drive a Jaguar, burn your frequent flier miles, or mooch about in a premium banking lounge.

But Africa's downtrodden masses are a far from unrewarding audience, if you but take the time to understand them. There are distinct motivations that drive the way poorer people live their lives. Obviously, one is day-to-day survival; it drives people who believe they cannot change things. In Africa, they only participate occasionally in the cash economy. Subsistence farming and barter are mainstays of their survival. They are guardians of tradition, preferring to reference earlier times – which always seemed better.

But at the same socio-economic level, we find people with a very different motivation. They are determined to escape from present circumstance. Let's call them 'Strugglers' and acknowledge that they are, by nature, optimists. They believe that every day will bring a fresh opportunity. They often leave home and take casual work far away, remitting much of what they earn to their family. They rise early and retire late; they work hard, physically. Their dawn and dusk are marked by long and hazardous travel. They seek solace in alcohol, in sex and in evangelical religion. They used to enjoy a single cigarette after work, until the World Health Organisation took that one small pleasure from them.

Strugglers look for the big chance: lotteries, promotions, and free offers. Many Marketers are still unaware that most sales promotion entries come from this group regardless of whether they use the brand or not! They are drawn to promotions by the possibility of escape from present circumstance. This is a rich seam for Marketers to mine.

Their frustrated material desire makes them crave flashy trainers, shiny cell phones and supersized audio systems. They watch sport and other big-crowd events because they live the life of the onlooker. Their time-constrained existence is fueled by junk food and quick fixes from sodas, sweets and snacks. They respond instinctively to bright colours and loud noise; Lingala music and preachers' amplified voices. Look at any daladala, matatu or taxi minibus crew in Africa and you are observing Strugglers at work.

These consumers are impulsive: they break the rules. The rapid upscaling of mobile phone networks in Africa was, in large part, thanks their appetite for empowerment. Successful Struggler brands are brash and rugged. They take the personality of the lovable rogue – charming and fun, but slightly devious. They never, never talk the consumer down. Instead they talk the world up.

Many years ago in East Africa, a large brewing group, who should have known better, launched an affordable beer brand. Its brand strapline was 'Bia Tosha', capable of the translation, 'Good enough for the likes of you'.

Its label was cheaply printed on matt paper, and the beer always came in the most scuffed bottles the bottling plant could find. It enjoyed initial success, but only amongst those who accepted that this was as good as beer could get. But Strugglers were embarrassed by its condescension. So much so that, in bars, they peeled off the label or turned the bottle round – so no one else could see the badge of shame.

When we (representing the commercial opposition) launched a competitor brand – with smart packaging and a proposition that encouraged people to be the best they could be – we forced it out of the market in less than a year. Marketing wins like that can be very satisfying!

First published September 2011

Let's Meet a
Targeting Expert

Rose Kimotho MBS

Rose Wairimu Kimotho is a media pioneer and entrepreneur with over 25 years' leadership experience in both advertising and media in Kenya. As a trail-blazer she has dedicated much of her career to building strong media brands that include Kameme FM, the first local language FM radio station, and K24 television, the first 24-hour news and information channel.

Rose is the Managing Director of 3 Stones TV – the first local language television channel. Prior this Rose founded Regional Reach, the company that operated community television sets for public viewing at 200 rural trading centres around the country. In recognition of her contribution towards the development of the broadcast sector in Kenya, Rose was awarded the Moran of the Burning Spear by the President of Kenya in 2003.

Before Rose ventured into entrepreneurship in 1994, she was General Manager of McCann Erickson in Kenya. She's a former Chairman of the Media Owners Association and non-executive Director of Stanbic Bank. She serves on the boards of Cytonn Investments; Population Services International and Rhino Ark. Rose was a member of the Attorney General's Task Force on Press Law. She holds a degree in Journalism from the University of Nairobi.

Rose's entire professional life has been spent in creating branded services for specific target audiences. She says: 'I believe that clearly defining the target group for a brand – a niche or group with common characteristics and interests – is the key part of any Marketing campaign. It enables one to determine how to position and where to market a brand. It inspires one to craft and focus the right message. In doing so, it makes for more effective and efficient campaigns.'

Chapter 5

Choosing Channels

In the decade that I have been writing about Marketing in Africa, two very significant changes have taken place in the world of media advertising. The first development has been enormously positive and beneficial. The second has been negative enough to undermine the credibility of Marketing as a profession on our continent.

The first was the digital media explosion. A global revolution, and the first in which African nations have participated on equal terms with the rest of the world. Having very limited access to technology before the 1990's we were suddenly liberated by the introduction of mobile telephone technology able to carry voice and data. In doing so we leapfrogged many decades of traditional market development and suddenly became very active in the online media space.

What a golden opportunity for Marketers! But, in fact, it was consumers who took control and made the most of this radical change. They began to choose who to listen to or view, and where and when to do it. They started to give the business world feedback on its products and services... on a scale and with an openness no one had ever imagined.

Established media channels were wrong-footed at every turn. Newspapers tried to digitise, but couldn't work out how to charge for it. TV stations failed to cope with the perfect storm of online streaming and satellite-delivered content. Broadcast became narrowcast, and broadcasters became downcast.

In tandem with this came the second development: Marketers abandoned media audience research. To be more accurate, few Marketers had ever supported regular countrywide media research. Few major advertisers were willing to pay for it, which is very strange. Audience research had begun with media monitoring services developed by Roger Steadman, a quintessential Marketing man who strongly objected to not getting the media space or airtime he had paid for. Rapidly it developed the ability to report on competitor media activity and then moved into measuring *audience delivery. All of which should have been 'meat and drink' to professional Marketers. Naturally most media channels hated being measured and each in turn tried to rubbish the results, but it was the Marketing community that allowed objective audience measurement to sicken and almost die. And what happens when you can't put an objective value to a media channel? You can only purchase it based on subjective measures, and that opens the door to corruption.*

While this chapter does give some pointers on how media channels should be selected for investment it mainly charts the rapid rise in importance of digital advertising and comments on how we all tried to make sense of it.

Channel planning

Marketing messages require the right channels to carry them to the eyes and ears of the target audience. Let's start with the basics: channel planning is the process of finding the most appropriate media channels in which your brand can engage consumers. It used to be called media planning, but the explosion of choices now available to Marketers seems to have necessitated a name change.

The Channel Planner is a person who works in the advertising agency environment and prepares channel recommendations for brand owners and managers. She proposes the best combination of media to achieve the given Marketing campaign objectives. This information then shapes the investment required and guides the creative process, as it determines the forms of advertising material to be produced: radio spots, online banners, event poster and so on. Doing this the other way around – by setting the budget or creating a TV commercial first – generally produces a sub-optimal result.

A good Channel Planner must answer a number of questions:

- Who am I trying to reach with my message; who is my target audience?
- How many of the target audience can I reach through paid-for media?
- Where do I prioritise the investment?
- Can I afford to target more than one audience?

- How frequently does my message need to appear? Some messages can be drip-fed over time, but a launch or promotion will demand high frequency repetition of message.

Luckily for Channel Planners in Kenya, we still have regular industry research to measure the audiences delivered by paid-for media. So here the Channel Planner's job has a statistical element, a rational analysis before more subjective criteria can be overlaid. We know, for example, how many people listen to Capital Radio at 07h15. We also know from what levels of society they are drawn.

Increasing numbers of markets on the Continent are developing similar industry research, and the process is to be lauded. Ghana is one of the leaders in understanding media consumption on the West African coast, thanks to effort and investment by media agency OMD. Sadly, without objective research measurement, media purchase is conducted on an informal and subjective basis. Money is spent depending on which media representative is more persistent; which magazine the client's wife reads or which outdoor supplier offers the sweetest inducement. Money is wasted, and some of it feeds corruption.

In a professional media agency, the Channel Planner starts with a blank piece of paper and builds her plan in a rational way. That then becomes part of the creative briefing discussion, and later part of a combined media and creative presentation to the client. In that meeting, the merits of both channel and message are debated and agreed. Here the interest of the client's brand is paramount.

In less professional media agencies there is a tendency to buy quantities of media space and airtime in advance and at a discount. Then to sell them on to clients at a premium. This is neither in the interest of the client, nor indeed of the development of media channels. It commoditises the whole process, and as a community we should resist this practice as strongly as possible.

There is no vocational training for channel planning. Candidates need to be numerate and analytical, but also creative. As Planners mature, negotiation skills become more important. If you are a good negotiator, you may eventually specialise in media trading – the purchase of planned media. That can be a stimulating career for the commercially savvy.

First published April 2012

How the Web affects brand reach

Recently I reviewed findings from BrandAssetValuator™ – the world's biggest database of brand health. I did this because here in Africa we are participating in the digital revolution on equal terms with the rest of the world. I noted two significant trends emerging from what we now call new media. These are Social and Mobile, and the importance lies in how they are converging.

Let's look today at how Social and Mobile are coming together. To contextualise this, the global average for social network penetration of a national population is already 52%. When I tell you that more Americans are on the Internet than have a passport, that won't surprise you – didn't they recently elect a President without a passport? And how about Twitter, the most powerful social media brand of the moment? It has already broken the barrier of 350 million tweets per day.

So, there is no longer any doubt that social media, for Marketers, must be the backbone of digital contact with consumers. It influences search, e-commerce, content and online communications. Some media experts even tell me that it now provides a cultural and behavioural overlay over the entire Internet. In other words, people are seeing the Worldwide Web through social media. So, when you spot a billboard (as I did today for Miller Genuine Draft beer) it is entirely appropriate that it features the call to action 'catch us on Facebook'.

In India, there are 33 million social media users, spending on average 13 hours a month on social sites. Imagine how that will climb when India follows Africa into broadband? Sorry, I couldn't resist that dig. We're always being told that India is the template for Africa and it's so not.

In America, a man called Eric Fisher has created an amazing image by plotting active Twitter and Flickr user locations. See it at **http://aphelis.net/eric-fisher-2011**. Apart from a mysterious blackout in America's Mid-West that runs from the Canadian border to Mexico, it looks like a night view of a totally electrified continent. I wish someone would do the same for Africa, because I am sure it would silence any doubt that we are part of the global trend.

So how is Mobile doing in the face of this onslaught? Very nicely, thank you. With over 5 billion handsets worldwide, and exponential growth in smartphones. Here in Africa we already know that anyone under 25 is accessing the Web through their phone. And, if mobile banking customers are due to reach 1.5 billion globally by 2015, guess how many will come in Africa? We lead the world in pioneering mass mobile finance solutions.

Marketers in Financial Services must be wondering how on earth they will control all these new customer relationships. Statement stuffers and mobile research questionnaires? Not likely. The truth is that these relationships will control and define them, and not the other way around. This must be an anxious time.

More people are now searching the web through mobile applications than through traditional search engines. Imagine that we already call Google and Yahoo traditional! Mobile music is now so prevalent in our culture that most up-to-date dictionaries no longer contain the words 'cassette tape'.

But here's one for the oldies. In the West, it's the over-55's who are adopting smartphone technology the fastest. That gels with the statistic that one in three Americans would rather give up sex than their smartphone!

First published February 2015

Embrace the Cloud

It's not often that Tech people get to discuss a subject that the rest of us are prepared to entertain. IT remains something of a Dark Art – peopled by the bright but uncommunicative. Fifteen years ago, they had our attention by suggesting a Doomsday scenario that their antecedents had failed to predict. Through our reliance on binary coding, they warned that we faced the imminent possibility that every computerised machine, environment or process would fail at one second past midnight on 31 December 1999.

For three years before that, they and their kin found themselves suddenly very important. Their numbers swelled to encompass people who had lost their relevance. These insignificant souls suddenly became Millennium Preparedness Experts. They were taken out, dusted down and given clipboards and committees with the mandate to ensure that their organisations were compliant. The problem was, no one knew what compliance meant. Not up until the final second, when it became clear that it had meant nothing.

For those three years, the IT community trod the corridors of power imbued with a sacerdotal significance. Then the day after dawned, and we didn't wake to a world of aircraft wrecks, crazed checkouts and seized lifts. Nothing had changed. In North Korea, the geeks would have been formed up and marched in front of the anti-aircraft guns.

So, it's no surprise that serious business has not yet embraced Cloud data storage. Globally the biggest reservations are about privacy and security. In human terms, that means that we don't quite trust it or the Tech people offering it. Personally, I think it would be quite fun, in response to a CFO's request for 10 years' audited accounts, to run into his office and shout: 'They're in the Cloud!' But not all businesspeople share my sense of humour.

As far as I can understand, the Cloud uses excess capacity in the global tech-sphere to store large amounts of data cheaply or free. I like to get to the benefit as soon as possible, particularly in matters of numeracy or technology. And the main benefit seems to be that most of us won't have to buy as much computer hardware as we used to.

To an SME, a home-based business or a freelancer, that is a significant boon. And I suspect it will be to bigger enterprises too. Here are some areas of Marketing activity that are already benefiting from the Cloud:

- Retail promotions, especially at peak sales times where customer and transaction data swells.
- Entertainment, where streaming is becoming the preferred way to enjoy audio, audio visual and gaming content.
- Truly entrepreneurially brands, where clever people see opportunities for high data businesses like Uber, Square, Chipotle and Amazon.

App creators and retailers must be prudent. A million personal medical files require more careful curation that the monthly accounts of a small business. But here and now in Africa, it's time to get on board and make the most of the Cloud as a place in which to do business.

First published June 2017

Retail turns full circle

Online shopping is growing at a phenomenal pace throughout the World. But in Africa, markets are still grappling with getting traditional brands to play in the Internet space. It's a tough business, because some brands may not yet be suited to that environment. Either in terms of their target audiences or brand positioning, or their ability to deal with the consumer conversations that will result.

Then there are the vested interests that create wheel spin. The IT department, the Procurement team and the Finance department, who all join forces to create inertia. In my experience, unless the Internet is a CEO priority, digitisation will proceed very slowly indeed. Which is a problem, because mobile Internet is fast becoming Africa's channel of choice.

Elsewhere in the world, some very big brands are facing other kinds of challenges. And, in the Retail sector, there's now real evidence that the wheel is now turning full circle with a move from virtual back into physical. Amazon, the world's greatest virtual store, is now planning to build a real 'bricks-and-mortar' one. In its 18 years of existence, Amazon has been delivering on its mission to be 'the Earth's most customer-centric company where people can find and discover anything they want to buy online'. Not an entirely new idea, but executed in a way that actually works. So, you might find it a bit 'off brand' to hear that they are seriously contemplating creating a physical store in the city of Seattle.

But perhaps it's a brilliant, innovative move for them – because we have to stop thinking that innovation and technology are one and the same thing. Innovation is about driving a brand story to customers through new channels. But not necessarily through digital ones. The Amazon brand has always offered consumers choice, cost and convenience. This good value for consumers has created enormous value for shareholders, especially during the current recession. Since 2008, Amazon's stock has almost quadrupled in value. Amazon is also about creating a sense of community, sharing reviews of products it stocks, lists that you can share, registers and reading recommendations.

So, while Amazon has succeeded beyond anyone's wildest expectations at being a virtual superstore, I think they are smart not to limit themselves to the Web. Amazon is a retail store and retail stores need to be where their consumers are. Remember the old retail mantra, 'location, location and location'? That means being online, but also on ground. Where their customers can interact, and engage in a different but equally important way.

Amazon the master retailer that became the master distributor has also now become Amazon the manufacturer. In widening the brand offering, they understand the need to expand the customer experience. So, what will the Amazon store be? A place to try out the Kindle and its offshoots? A store with an inventory that's based on aggregated purchase data gathered from Amazon customers in the area? A Walmart with virtual items that you buy online, but sample in a physical space – assisted by an army of Amazons?

First published December 2017

Life, love and death online

There's a huge amount of writing about social media these days, and it's shifting from technical explanation to observation of the behavioural trends in this new and powerful space. The more Marketers become accustomed to it, the more we can see that it's a place that reflects many aspects of the human condition. And to know humanity is the first step to being an effective Marketer.

A couple of years ago a much-admired friend and colleague of mine suddenly died. He was one of the freshest advertising thinkers I have ever met, and he wrote a huge amount of inspiring material that was published online and in smart glossy brochures. He had a gift for making business writing intelligible and attractive. His name was Simon Silvester. He took a year off to travel and enjoy himself, and one night in Greece he went to sleep and he never woke up. He was in his early 40's.

I mention him now, not solely to acknowledge his memory, but because he still exists on Facebook. And that disturbed me for some time, raising the question of what one should if a friend or loved one, active on social media, passes on.

The answer is that Facebook now has a protocol for addressing death. They call it Memorializing – a process that enables validated family members to choose whether keep the page going, in memoriam, or to delete it. It gives people the emotional permission to visit his page and remember.

Having touched upon death, let's contrast it with a look at social media and life. Specifically, how social media is contributing to human procreation. Many of you know that the online space has become a facilitator of social sexual engagement. From online dating, to Apps that allow you to find men or women in your immediate vicinity who are open to 'fun, laughter and perhaps something more.' Tinder is for the heterosexual community and Grinder for the gay, and both highly successful in terms of audience engagement. In the days of Armistead Maupin, San Franciscan gays used to pick each other up over the supermarket fruit counter.

Now on Grinder they can scroll through pictures and messages advertising same-sex partners who are immediately available. I'm too old and too married for Tinder, but I believe it delivers the same benefit to straight people.

In Iceland, folk have taken to App design to address a related yet different problem. There are only 320,000 Icelanders, and their country attracts almost no immigration. That represent a very shallow gene pool, which has genetic consequences if you take dating to the next stage.

So, the ever-practical Icelanders have developed an App to guard against unintended incest. This is based upon a national study that was originally designed to help people to trace their family trees. But now, if Bjork meets Sven (names changed to protect the guilty) they can bump smartphones to discover how closely they are related. The technology is almost as calculating as a prenuptial agreement. Yesterday I described this challenge and its tech solution to a Kenyan Sales Director and he was more pragmatic about the whole thing: 'Why don't the Icelanders get some Africans in? That would solve the problem.' He does have a point.

First published March 2011

Here are 5 tips to inform your approach to channels

▶ Channel Planning Tip 1 – buy research

I have spent a great deal of time in the company of Market Researchers, and I wish more Marketers would do the same. In Kenya, we are spoiled by the choice of research suppliers and techniques available to inform our Marketing efforts. But I don't think we make full use of them.

This week, the Kenya Advertising Research Foundation hosted a breakfast meeting to brief Marketers on the latest round of industry media research. This is independent, objective data on who in Kenya reads which newspapers, listens to which radio stations and watches which TV channels. Even the burgeoning growth of Internet access and online time is measured. This information has been available to Marketers, intermittently, for decades. But it recently became more regular – thanks to the collaborative efforts of far-sighted leaders in the Advertising Practitioners Association; fewer than 20 Marketing clients; and a professional research company named Synovate. Soon it will be better still, with the introduction of People Meters which allow us to automatically track media consumption habits on a continuous basis.

So how did the marketplace greet such a useful study? Well, firstly everyone enjoyed the breakfast, judging by the number of second helpings taken. Secondly the audience nodded and listened appreciatively. Then we had questions, some of which were constructive but most seemed to try to pick holes in what had been presented.

The audience did contain several representatives of the media industry, who tend to enter audience research debriefs with teeth bared. Ready to lash out at the first negative statistic about their own publication or station. But it wasn't just the media reps whose minds began closing like sluice gates as the information flowed towards them. There were Marketers too. Using that annoying tactic of looking clever by rubbishing other people's hard work. Very few of them had actually paid to belong to the study.

Let's take a quick look at some of the tasty information morsels that dropped onto the table during breakfast:

- Kenya is a much more urban society than it was 12 years ago (36% versus 24%)
- Kenyans are becoming more affluent, there are many more members of LSM groups 1-8.
- Radio listenership is slightly down, TV viewing is up
- On TV, viewership is increasing for soaps, reality and comedy
- Citizen TV and radio currently dominate the broadcast airways
- Internet usage per head of population has increased from 37% (2007) to 81% (2011)
- Under 25s access the Internet through their phones, over 25's from computers.

These are simply top line results, but this audience research is so cleverly built that it can be mined very deeply. Internet usage can be correlated with radio usage to build a clearer picture of young media habits. The decline of printed media can be analysed by age group, by sex, by region and so on and so forth. Advertising Agencies also have additional software to ask questions specific to your brand's target audience. This is information that many African markets will take decades to develop; others will never achieve it. We have it in Kenya, and every Brand Manager worth his salt should be familiar with it.

First published May 2011

▶ Channel Planning Tip 2 – share with care

In Africa, our natural amiability and sociability make us suckers for social media. The Facebook, LinkedIn and Twitter gross numbers continue to rise every month. People hook up with each other, with their leaders and with brands. It's a great space for Marketers, but we're still not using it with the confidence that we should.

I think confidence is important. Anyone who has ever learnt to ride a horse will tell you that you must let the beast know who is in charge. Pilots will tell you that flying is all about being several steps ahead of the aircraft – so that you have positive control. It's a lesson many African motorists should heed: daily I am surprised by numbers of my fellow drivers, who are clearly enjoying the ride but don't have much influence over velocity or direction. It's the same with social media. If you use it for your brand, use it positively and impose your own direction.

Online we are global, so that means we are surrounded by many examples of positive control in social media. And also by brands who have let social media get away from them. When AirAsia lost an aircraft last year, CEO Tony Fernandes made powerful use of Twitter as his first line of briefing for journalists and customers. Being Chairman of London soccer side Queen's Park Rangers, Mr. Fernandes has taken time to develop his social media confidence in less critical surroundings. AirAsia's briefing strategy showed a maturity that would give African carriers pause for thought. On this continent, airlines have been known to address an aircraft loss with a flurry of contradictory messaging followed by a heavy effort at condolence. Followed by a complete silence as they wait for the story to go away.

Global logistics brand UPS bases its relationships with business on social media. Building a community around the brand, giving advice on how on-time delivery can help small businesses and encouraging customers to share their delivery experiences. It's a lesson other courier brands could learn from. Last month it took me 3 weeks and approximately 12 hours of office time to validate the fact that DHL had in fact delivered two important letters for me. I'm not sure what the DHL brand promise is but in Kenya their staff members haven't bought into it.

Candace Kuss, Director of Social Media at PR agency Hill & Knowlton in London says that some of her business-to-business clients are doing pioneering work on LinkedIn. Norway's Statoil created a page to highlight its thought leadership on energy innovation and attracted 21,000 global influencers. Kuss says, 'For B2B, I think we are seeing the renaissance of the company blog as an 'owned' social hub and white papers blossoming anew as interactive data visualisations.' Translating the PR talk, this means that original thinking attributable your brand should now appear on social media in the form of downloadable PDFs, links to your YouTube channel and podcasts. The challenge is to create some original thinking that other people will want to read!

Social media used weakly, without confidence or forethought, can be disastrous. Publishing house Penguin discovered this when they Tweeted the hashtag **#YourMum**. Their intention was to encourage dialogue about the books mothers might like to receive on Mother's Day. But to children, Your Mum is the cue for an endless round of playground jokes. Plenty of rude Tweets followed, and **#YourMum – she can easily be seen from Antarctica** was one of the kinder ones. High-end UK supermarket chain Waitrose put up the hashtag **#Waitrosereasons** and asked Twitters to finish the sentence, 'I shop at Waitrose because...'.

This provoked a derisive reaction across social media, giving people the chance to attack the brand for its high prices and affluent customer base. There was much humorous discussion about Waitrose being the best place to buy gold loo paper and unicorn food. A typical Tweet read, 'I shop at Waitrose because it makes me feel important, and I absolutely detest being surrounded by poor people.'

I'm not highlighting these social media winners and losers to put Marketers off the channel. Instead my advice is to use social media like you mean it. Be businesslike, plan ahead and manage the discussion that you intend to stimulate. Social media is a business communications channel, so let's get more professional about using it.

First published July 2014

▶ Channel Planning Tip 3 – beware viral

Sometimes you look back and you wonder at how you became connected with an idea or a person – the chances seem so infinitesimally small. Five months ago, I met a security contractor in our office car park. He's one of a growing band of serious, experienced men who were once military and now play a role securing strategic installations in Africa. He asked me whether I had heard about Applied Memetics, but I had not. So, I looked on the Internet and discovered that the term has recently come to be applied to the spread of doctrine in post-conflict environments. Hence, the interest of the serious gentleman and his comrades.

Memetics, as a phrase, was coined by Richard Dawkins in his 1976 book 'The Selfish Gene'. In it, Dawkins suggests that ideas, or units of culture – memes – are very much like genes in the way they grow and succeed. Memes are hosted in the minds of individuals, and their success is measured by how well they jump from mind to mind. Dawkins also suggested that, as with genetics, a meme's success may lie in contributing to the success of its host. If you are reading this with a hangover or the mid-week blues, I do apologise. It may seem complicated, but there is a point here that is related to Marketing. Marketing is about the spread of ideas, that lead to new habits that in turn create commercial activity. Thanks to Marketing, people consider new stuff, try it and buy it. In this way, market-led economies develop.

Memetics is notable for sidestepping any concerns about the truth of ideas and beliefs. Instead, it is primarily interested in their success. So, Marketers with the power to influence millions carry a weighty responsibility. I hesitate to call it moral, but it is certainly a responsibility to do the right thing by your brand and your consumers. I think professional Marketers need to consider a couple of points when spreading ideas. These come from Dan Zarella, a social media scientist. See **www.danzarella.com**

First point: even the most virulent of viral Marketing campaigns can leave a brand or product right where it started. It takes hard work to seed the message in the right place. And it's even harder to get the tonality right. Although we remain surrounded by people who believe in broadcasting messages, smarter Marketers understand that persuasion is stronger than promulgation.

Second point: it's a myth that for an idea or branded message to go viral it has to be great. Sadly, human nature attracts us just as strongly to negative memes. The list of widely adopted bad ideas is endless, but here's a small sample:

- Terrorism
- Suicide
- Drug abuse
- Anti-Semitism
- Pyramid schemes
- Religious cults

Marketers, please take care to shape the right online messages for your brands.

First published February 2015

▶ Channel Planning Tip 4 – be discreet

I now want to touch on an aspect of channel usage that most people discount. It's how you, as an individual, appear on social media, and how much you should share. I start with a signal reminder: 'Facebook is for life.'

In our rush to declare our individuality; and use the voice that social media has finally given us, we are often reckless. We share too openly and we treat social media as a broad pasture across which we canter, showering all of our latest news and personal information with gay abandon. How many of us consider using different social media for different purposes? For example, Facebook for friends and family only. LinkedIn for business networking. Twitter for broader conversations. It really is time to be deliberate about our personal exposure on social media because, once it's there, it never goes away.

My grandmother used to have a saying about ladies who wore low-cut dresses: 'If it's not for sale, it shouldn't be in the shop window.'

Let's modify that axiom to: "If it's not for the permanent record, it shouldn't be on the Internet.'

Sharing your latest romantic intrigues will prove to be embarrassing later on. Filling your Facebook page with fun pictures of drunken parties can lose you that future job opportunity, because Facebook is now one of the first places employers go to validate a seemingly perfect candidate. Some sharing will actually put you in harm's way, because we now live in a world overshadowed by terror. Do you really want to leave details of family, addresses or regular patterns of behaviour for evil-doers to browse?

It's now time to calm down a bit. Become more selective, less competitive. If you want to impress people, remember the maxim 'less is more'. Truly confident people don't have to tell you how clever or socially active they are.

Now, when I mentioned that posts never go away, that wasn't strictly true anymore. The latest news about social media is a landmark ruling by the European Court of Justice. Two people recently applied to Google to have details of their past removed from Internet search results. Last Tuesday, the Court ruled that anyone could demand that information about them be removed from search engines. This enshrines in law the 'right to be forgotten.'

Although the new ruling will not facilitate the removal of news articles, blogs or posts it could force search engines to remove the links to the content, thereby making the content impossible to access. As Russia moves towards a repeat of the Stalinist era, I wonder whether Mr. Putin has heard this news and rejoiced?

First published August 2016

▶ Channel Planning Tip 5 – be human

Isn't the imagination a wonderful thing? This weekend I felt the power of imagination while reading the obituary of the American novelist Ray Bradbury, and it spurred me to buy a collection of his short stories.

My goodness, what a brain, and what a worker! Living proof that success is part inspiration, part perspiration. He wrote 27 novels and over 600 published short stories. His work has been translated into 36 languages and been the subject of films, stage plays and TV series. Bradbury wrote eerie short stories that touched upon horror, and he opened people's eyes to science fiction. He wrote about the future colonisation of Mars, and imagined innovations like giant screen televisions, cash dispensers and microwave ovens. All this from a man who never learnt to drive a car, never used lifts, and thought that the Internet was a waste of time.

And in his footsteps, technologists continue to innovate and consumers to adopt far faster than Marketers seem to grasp. A little over a year ago Amazon, a major Cloud storage provider, had a problem. The loss of their system created serious downtime for a number of businesses and caused some of them long-term damage. It took Amazon two full days to explain, and this was their basic statement of cause: '*As with any complicated operational issue this one was caused by several root causes interacting with one another.*'

Snappy response. But wait, it got worse. In a letter sent to affected businesses, Amazon wrote:

'*A few days ago, we sent you an email letting you know that we were working on recovering an inconsistent data snapshot of one or more of your Amazon EBS volumes. We are very sorry, but ultimately our efforts to manually recover your volume were unsuccessful. The hardware failed in such a way that we could not forensically restore the data. What we were able to recover has been made available via a snapshot, although the data is in such a state that it may have little to no utility. We apologize for this volume loss and any impact to your business. Sincerely, Amazon Web Services, EBS Support.*'

That is poor customer service gone mad. A failure of critical technology compounded by an outrageously indifferent attitude.

Sci-Fi author Arthur C. Clarke once wrote: 'Any sufficiently advanced technology is indistinguishable from magic.'

I think it's time we put the magic back into customer relationships, particularly for technology products and services.

First published March 2016

Let's meet a
Choreographer of Channels

Lenny Ng'ang'a

Lenny N'gang'a is the CEO of the Omnicom media group in East Africa, which comprises two leading media agency brands – Saracen OMD and Saracen PHD – and operates in Kenya, Uganda and Tanzania.

He holds a degree in Political Science and Philosophy from the University of Nairobi as a base upon which he has layered multiple professional courses in advertising and leadership. Lenny co-founded Saracen OMD in 2002, and PHD in 2007.

Prior to taking his entrepreneurial leap of faith, he worked for giant global advertising agencies Ogilvy & Mather and McCann Erickson, where he created and executed communications strategies across East and West Africa. He has worked across most Sub-Saharan Africa markets, earning the HK McCann Global Leadership Award for his passion in media along the way, as well as managing multi-country businesses for over 19 years. Lenny served as the Chairman of the Association of Practitioners in Advertising and has served as Chairman of the Oversight Committee of the Kenya Audience Research foundation since 2010.

Lenny says: 'Channel planning sets the crucial pathway that gets your message to your target audience. Get it wrong and you're throwing good money after bad. Get it right and the reward is a positive return on investment. Provided, of course, that your message is on point with the audience!'

Chapter 6

Getting Creative

"It may well be that creativity is the last unfair advantage we're legally allowed to take over our competitors." So wrote the father of modern advertising, Bill Bernbach.

But it is surprising how a continent like Africa, jammed full of the most inspiring creative talent, rarely expresses commercial creativity in its Marketing content.

Advertising creativity began under European influence in the Africa of the 1960's. The three centres for advertising development were Lagos, Nairobi and Johannesburg. All advertising content was Anglocentric and everyone looked to London for inspiration.

When I arrived in Kenya in the early 1990's, the East African scene was dominated by expatriate creative Directors from the English-speaking world. Britons, Australians and even Canadians employed scores of local people and some made genuine efforts to develop local talent. One or two Kenyans and Ugandans grew to take senior positions in creative departments, but they were very much the exception. In the 2000's the ad scene became dominated by Indian-run companies and the door shut on large-scale development of local talent. Thankfully, smaller agencies continued to encourages the buds of local creativity but it wasn't really until the digital revolution, at the end of that decade, that local creative content began to flourish again.

Local attitudes to young people following a creative career didn't help matters, either. Hard-working mums and dads are still horrified if their proto-lawyer, doctor or accountant comes home one day and announces a desire to direct art, write copy or play music. Today, young creatives still have to be quite determined to break these social taboos. More worrying, the past twenty years in East Africa has seen the emergence of a Marketing peer group that doesn't take creativity seriously or see its true commercial potential. Worse still, they imagine that they are creative enough to tackle most day-to-day creative projects themselves and consequently begrudge paying for specialist help.

This is a state of affairs that you are unlikely to find on any other continent. I really do believe that it is holding back the development of our economies, so I take the opportunity to champion the value of ideas whenever I can. This chapter provides me with one such opportunity.

Creativity is all about persuasion

I meet many young Marketers. In fact, most Marketers in Africa are young, which reflects the inherent truth about our continent's population. Being young, what they lack in experience they make up for with enthusiasm. But enthusiasm alone cannot carry the day for Marketing as a profession, or for Marketers as career professionals. For the world is a hard place, and commercial competition now exists in Africa as never before. The sad truth is that Africa lacks tertiary education opportunities in Marketing-related subjects. South Africa is best provided for. But, even there, the choice of really competitive Marketing schools is very limited.

Who am I to complain? My own generation were very much generalists, who had an aptitude for Marketing and learned on the job. I myself was educated to be an archaeologist and historian. Perhaps the skills I learnt in those fields have helped me to decipher convoluted briefs, unearth consumer insights and curate learnings from past campaigns!

First and foremost, a Marketing communications professional must be a persuader. If you can't argue your own case, you're sure as heck not going to convert a target audience. In 1957, Vance Packard wrote a seminal work on advertising which disturbed his generation. 'The Hidden Persuaders' revealed for the first time the psychological techniques that the ad industry used to make consumers want to buy goods. More recently Martin Lindstrom, an advertising industry veteran of countless McDonalds, Microsoft and P&G campaigns, has published 'Brandwashed: Tricks Companies Use to Manipulate Our Minds and Persuade Us to Buy'. Although separated by half a century, these books reveal that what it takes to be successful in Marketing hasn't fundamentally changed. But the power of Marketing has increased exponentially.

Marketers have more information about potential customers than ever before. Every time you use a loyalty card, you surrender personal information. Professional data miners use electronic data to create a detailed picture of what you have bought in the past (history sniffing) and how you bought it (behaviour sniffing). They can then draw your attention to products they think you might want to buy in the future.

Marketers probe the behavioural sciences for insights. For example, studies show that music can affect people's behaviour. Shoppers in large stores who are exposed to piped tunes with a slow tempo spend 18% longer in the store and make 17% more purchases than those who shop in silence. Marketers are also devoting more effort to wooing children. The average American three-year-old can recognise 100 brands. Many can also recite ad jingles more readily than their times tables.

Here in Africa, Marketers are now devoting much more effort to Marketing to men or, as Mr Lindstrom puts it, getting men to shop like women. African men are style and status conscious. Where their fathers might have splashed out on the occasional deodorant, the average urban male has an armoury of cosmetic canisters on his bathroom shelf.

Marketers understand that the most powerful persuader is peer pressure. And social media makes it easier for them to start social epidemics. In New York, the Eagle Outfitters' Times Square store flashes pictures of anyone buying its products live onto a 25-storey screen. Then it scoops free publicity as these instant celebrities send the images to their friends. Marketers also create armies of brand ambassadors: Apple hires students to become Apple Campus Reps and turns entire sections of university book shops into mini Apple stores.

Now, here's the challenge. In Africa, as in the West 70 years ago, many of these Marketing techniques run counter to socially acceptable behaviour. So, Marketers, whom we acknowledge as young and relatively inexperienced, are caught in a difficult place. Many of them know the kinds of activities they should be conducting for their brands, but are often incapable of articulating them to their seniors.

I'd like to see them win their first battles over audience segmentation. You can't hope to persuade everybody, so choose a target audience, and define it well. Address it through media channels that don't waste your budget; and maximise message impact through relevant creativity. Understand that persuading an audience of four million people is better than failing to interest an audience of forty million.

First published October 2016

Prize creative ideas over process

Over the last fifteen years, African Marketers have become quite good at execution. At copying ideas from other markets and assimilating global techniques; and gaining international qualifications in managing process.

Often specialist expertise pops up in places you'd least expect. Senegal has a funky Tech culture. Botswana, although small, has a highly connected and worldly business community. Nigeria is a place where you can get big things done, fast ... but often in ways you couldn't predict!

Right now, African commercial and constitutional legislature is moving towards an acceptance of the value of ideas, and the notion that ideas can be owned. That's a slow journey, on a continent where wealth must be visible to be real. But I believe our inability to place a value on concepts, or assign ownership to ideas, is detrimental to further progress.

People in the advertising business still encounter young Marketing clients who think creative ideas are bit silly. Not serious enough to add value to their professional status. How wrong they are.

Surely it's a greater weakness to trivialise notions that are as yet unrealised? Just as it's foolish to squash campaign plans just because the results lie in the future and cannot be precisely predicted.

I suspect that far too many young Marketers in Africa are riding the execution curve. Focusing on process over persuasion; confusing activity for productivity. Every CEO I know attends Marketing meetings where presenters invite them to see 'what's been keeping us busy'. But they don't care what's been keeping you busy; they want to know what has been achieved!

CEOs want to hear: 'We discovered that business journalists were rubbishing our new product because they didn't understand it. So, we held face-to-face briefings with ten lifestyle journalists and invited them to trial it at home. After three weeks, we have generated six photo opportunities and four endorsements in lifestyle articles.'

Instead CEOs often get: 'Well, first we briefed the PR agency on the challenge. They were a bit slow coming back, but when they did we created press packs, which contained the product pictures and a write-up. Then we booked the venue. Then we organised for the press to be invited. Then.....'

By which time the average CEO is climbing the walls.

This fixation on process is making many CEOs fear that the new generation of Marketers are ideas averse. There are many Marketers in Africa who are not young. Many of them have their own businesses these days, and are generating and executing business ideas of their own. Does this mean they were better educated or trained? Were they encouraged to experiment and develop their own initiatives, rather than relying on academic learning-by-rote? Did they interact with creative agencies of a higher calibre? Or is it simply an issue of maturity? Whatever it is, mature Marketers are increasingly critica of the younger generation. More so, because they are now having to sell them new ideas about research, online media, promotional concepts and customer experience.

On their behalf, I'd like to encourage CEOs to identify and promote Marketing people who rate ideas over process. People who take calculated risks, rather than follow category norms. Who prize insights and hunches; and are bold enough to admit mistakes and learn from them. Because, without bold ideas, Marketing can only create limited value.

First published May 2012

Creativity needs a call to action

Businesses must have a purpose; and brands must have a call to action. Without the former, employees have no direction. Without the latter, customers have no reason to buy.

Business Purpose is the most important output of business strategy. It's the bold ambition you set for your company, something you really want to win at. A clear ambition that defines everything the company does: from the markets in which it chooses to operate to the products it will offer. It makes sense of the capabilities to be developed and the strategic partnerships to be sought.

Then, when you shape a Brand Promise, you package your Business Purpose to make it relevant to your chosen target audiences. Finding a place for it in their lives and promising a value that means something to them. Senior teams often make the mistake of assuming their staff will know how to act when it comes to delivering the Brand Promise. That potential customers will know how to respond to Marketing messages. So Marketers need to come up with a clear call to action.

That is where the slogan comes in. A slogan should not be a random attempt to bamboozle the public; an over-promise or a downright lie. A slogan must be a call to action. Interestingly, that's the etymology of the word slogan. First recorded in sixteenth century Scotland, slogan was the Gaelic expression *sluagh-ghairm*. *Sluagh* meaning army, and *gairm* meaning cry. Literally a war cry – used to rally the clan before battle.

So, was the first slogan 'Freedom!' from the movie Braveheart? Probably not. But for any war cry to work it must strike a chord with its audience; address a fundamental need and incite a specific action. For a slogan to direct action it cannot be ambiguous. At the Battle of Waterloo, Napoleon was not defeated by superior forces, but by ambiguity. He left his orders open to interpretation, so a vital part of his army headed off in the wrong direction.

Coca-Cola has always been good at slogans. 'Taste the feeling' is the current one; it directs an action and promises an effect.

Nike's 'Just do it' has inspired several generations of surprisingly un-athletic people. In fact, today Nike's brand strategy defines an athlete as anyone who has body!

Advertising I spotted recently for Two Rivers, one of East Africa's most ambitious shopping developments, risks ironic interpretation with its: 'Two good to be true.' But the worst slogan I have yet seen was for a glass-making company, commanding its customers to: 'Come to us for all your glazing requirements – because we don't know any better.'

First published November 2017

How to judge creative ideas

Let's put ourselves in the shoes of a CEO. It's hard being one: moving from the certainty of your particular area of specialisation to the anxiety of a wider ambit. Being asked to make judgements on aspects of the business you have never considered before, and may not fully understand.

One of the hardest areas to grasp seems to be Marketing, despite the fact that we all have a passing acquaintance with the discipline. We all consume advertising. Deny it if you like, but then go into your bathroom and tell me why this toothpaste or that shampoo brand is on your shelf. We are all afflicted by promotions, mostly for brands we would never otherwise consider. We all enjoy sponsorship of our golf competitions and art exhibitions.

We notice the impact of PR as we read our newspaper, watch TV news or browse a magazine. Often, we are aware that the editorial message has been influenced by a brand. So, at the CEO level, everyone is aware of the power of commercial messaging.

But it's different when the CEO's considered opinion is sought by his own Marketing team. How on earth should he judge the ideas they present; how much should he direct their plans? The easiest (and worst) way is to abdicate responsibility.

One bank CEO admitted to me that he had no idea how to judge his Marketing Manager's proposals, so he 'bowed to her professional judgement.' This turned out to be an error, as her media investment was being influenced by bribery. It took him a year to find that out.

Advertising can make the CEO a hero or a laughing stock. So, what should the CEO look for when his team come to him with new ideas? I defer to a mentor of mine, Adrian Holmes*. Here are the questions he would ask in any Marketing presentation:

1. *Does the team have ownership of the advertising idea?* Are they pitching it as if it was their own idea, or are they mumbling something about 'this is what the Agency has come up with'? If it is the former, lend them your ear as they clearly believe in what they are showing you. If it's the latter, send them away.

2. *Is there a clear idea in the advertising they show you?* If there is, you'll get it straight away. If they have to explain it, you should worry. If they start to use jargon on you, send them away. Demand that your message is clear before it is clever.

3. *Does the work seem familiar?* Contrary to many people's instincts, this is a warning sign. If you work in insurance, and the advertising idea makes you feel comfortable, it may mean your team are following category convention. The colours will reassure you and the images will seem familiar because your team are benchmarking themselves against what the rest of the category is saying. Advertising ideas that make you feel comfortable are unlikely to stand out from the crowd. Ideas that make you feel faintly uneasy are the ones you should encourage.

4. *Is this more than a one-off?* Advertising does not work in small doses. The best advertising has an idea that can carry

on for years, and give birth to innumerable fresh expressions. In a successful campaign, individual ads are like the verses of a popular hymn. But, too often, CEOs are asked to judge a one-off advertisement in isolation.

As Adrian would say, bad advertising goes up like a rocket, but comes down like a stick.

Adrian Holmes was the Executive Creative Director of Young & Rubicam EMEA, when I worked with him. During his distinguished career, he won numerous creative awards at festivals all over the world, including Cannes, D&AD, The One Show and the Campaign Press Awards. His work has inspired Heineken, Stella Artois, Plymouth Gin, Hamlet, HSBC, Saab, Vauxhall, Citroen, Nestlé, Albany Life and British Army Officer Recruitment. In 1994 Adrian served as President of D&AD.

First published May 1997

The human face of advertising

As a Marketer, I am profoundly interested in content. And I believe that there's a big difference between what advertisers say and what consumers receive. It's a difference all Marketers need to understand, because we've all seen too much poor advertising in Africa. The quarter page press ad that attempts to make twenty copy points. The billboard that features the brand logo five times, and insists on carrying all the office phone numbers, too. The TV commercial that looks so cheap that it actually devalues the brand it's trying to promote.

No Brand Manager should take pride in filling every centimetre of bought space or showing every variant of the product pack. Instead, they should be worried that no-one will even see their ad, much less retain all that information. People read what interests them, and then only retain a small percentage of it. If you want them to retain more then you have to be prepared to do two things:

Make your message relevant: address it to a target audience – a carefully selected part of the total population – and couch it in language that appeals to them.

Make your offer relevant: either in what your product does, or how it makes them feel. If you want to hit the jackpot, you need both.

Marketers today face many challenges in addressing specific audiences; and most of those challenges exist within their own company. Senior management always tends to demand a broader focus. They make comments like: 'Yes the Youth is important. But let's not alienate existing middle-aged customers.' This places the Marketer on the horns of a dilemma.

Then, when it comes to the actual messaging content, senior managers are prone to dumbing things down. They like their advertising to reflect an imagined reality: the smiling family around the meal table; the proud mum with her sparkling loo. Which explains why so many African advertising campaigns use hackneyed images of grinning consumers as the centre of all visual communication. It's been the paradigm here for over 50 years, and here's how it is done:

You book a photographer and gather up a whole family of healthy-looking consumers. Clean them up and dress them in new clothes. Try to feature your brand colours in their wardrobe, that's a clever touch. Then get them to hold your product, or stand next to it and make them grin. Not smile wistfully, not laugh uproariously, just force an embarrassed rictus.

Marketers who create this kind of advertising obviously hope people will think, "Look at them, they are very happy with Brand X.' But most people don't think anything at all when they see this kind of communication, because it is simply wallpaper.

According to David B. Givens, Director of the USA's Center for Nonverbal Studies, the face is 'every human's visual trademark. A powerful expression of attitudes, opinions, and moods that defines our identity and enables us to communicate and connect without words'. So, as connecting with consumers becomes ever more difficult, please let's have fewer cheesy grins in African advertising.

First published February 2000

Here are 5 tips to improve brand creativity

▶ Creativity Tip 1 – we all deserve better TV ads

When I first came to Kenya 25 years ago, we had limited media choice but much higher standards of creativity in advertising.

I don't mean the kind of boutique self-indulgence that immature creative people try to get away with. I mean commercial communication that makes people sit up and behave differently. We used to produce television advertising that was the equal of anything on this continent, and in many cases better than the work created in South Africa. We had strong creative leaders, good production facilities and rich musical and acting talent. We also had clients who believed in the power of the TV medium.

Last month, I sat down with 30 young Kenyans to review the TV commercials currently airing in this market. We devised a simple rating system. We watched each commercial and then individually rated it from 1-5 (where 1 was excellent and 5 was weak) on whether it contained an idea, and on how well produced it was. Let me clarify those criteria:

If a TV commercial has an idea, it makes something better than a bald claim. For example, Commercial Bank of Africa's campaign 'What stress-free banking is all about' featured a psychiatrist counselling a patient, who ends up himself being counselled about his own choice of bank. That TV commercial has an idea.

By contrast, 'Bank of Bogoria. Voted best bank in East Africa, by other bankers' does not have an idea.

Our second criterion was one of production value. High production values are what you achieve when you decide to invest proper money in a TV commercial. They buy the right camera format, the subtlest lighting and clearest sound quality. They fund intelligent casting and inspired wardrobe. They invariably produce a piece of communication that looks great and is watchable for several years.

Unfortunately, neither Marketers or Accountants tend to view investment in TV production as an enduring asset with a cost that can be amortised over time. Instead they focus on the lowest possible production cost at the time of commissioning. So, they end up producing unwatchable ads.

How did fifty of the current TV commercials perform in our little evaluation? Sadly, it was much harder to find a commercial that had an idea than one with good production values. Only two commercials of the fifty rated a score above 5. A nice spot for Nivea for Men had an idea that dramatised how men might cool their shaving rash if they didn't have Nivea to hand. And a Nokia animated commercial had less of an idea, but excellent digital animation which partly made up for it. That, sadly, was that.

I reckon we have a long way to go, to get back to 15 years ago. To a time when local TV commercials had real bang for buck, even if there were only 2 channels to air them on. We still have all those creative talents and resources available to us.

But what we have nearly lost is the will to use creativity to commercial advantage.

First published February 2014

▶ Creativity Tip 2 – avoid DIY radio

Last week, I heard a plaintive cry from a creative person. I will not identify him with anything more than the letter M. But I will reveal that is a creative person in a national radio station: the resource many Marketers use to produce their radio commercials. He began in dramatic fashion: *'It is with deep regret that we announce the death of creativity in the Kenyan advertising industry.'*

First rule of copywriting, capture their attention in the first sentence. But is was no ordinary funeral announcement, as M is clear that murder has been committed. The suspects are Brand Managers and the charge is as follows: *'All one has to do is listen to a radio station or look at the billboards around town or an ad in the paper to realise that there's always similarity in the ads and promotions running across this country.'*

M highlights the heinous crime of category convention. This occurs when many players in a category all advertise in the same way: *'Every promotion has some form of a Sheng name to it, not because it works for their brand but because it was successful for another brand and it sounds nice.'*

Harsh words, but wait till you hear what he says about Brand Managers' briefing skills: *'In the radio world, the turnaround time for every brief is at most a day, and the brief is usually ridiculous.'* For example, a brief for a radio promo might read, *'We need a catchy name for our new exciting promotion, something similar to what Brand A had but catchier, something to turn heads. I don't know what, but you are the pro! So, come up with something by lunchtime as we have to launch the promotion this afternoon.'*

Most CEOs might find this hard to believe, knowing that they have recruited their Brand Managers to be properly prepared, analytical and systematic. But, according to M, worse is yet to come: *'So the creative person does his level best to come up with something amazing in 2-3 hours, only to be told that the Marketing*

Director and the other Managers didn't quite feel the vibe. So, they decided to come up with the idea themselves and write the ad, plus the name of the promotion!'

As a creative person, who is passionate about his intellectual property, M is scathing about the end result: *'A shamelessly long disaster, playing on your radio for 3 months. A spot that everyone either ignores by turning off, or makes the butt of all jokes in offices, on street corners and in bars countrywide...'*

M's accusation is that the creative ability to present offerings in new and different ways is in danger of becoming commoditised. But less than a decade ago, when commercial radio first came to Kenya, Capital FM was radically different from the state broadcaster. Kameme FM did a similar job for regional audiences. Kiss FM, Classic FM and QFM all invested in differentiating themselves by audience, content and tonality. But modern Marketers seem to have forgotten that radio advertising should be part of the entertainment experience. The same is true of television, but no one watching free-to-air TV in Africa would describe ad breaks as entertaining.

If African Marketers continue to downplay the value of creative content in advertising, fewer consumers will be engaged by entertaining commercials that make them like the brand. And here comes the sucker punch: in five years' time most broadcast material in Africa will be streamed through the Internet, and consumers will self-select content. So where will your mobile airtime pricing, margarine promotions and caring bank ads be then? They will be lost in the Ether.

First published May 2010

▶ Creativity Tip 3 – fewer billboards

I am on record as saying we would all be better off if there were no more than eight billboard sites in Nairobi, and a proportionate number in other towns and cities. Coming from a former Adman, most people felt this statement smacked of insanity.

That's because most people think an Adman's job is to make money from Marketers by selling them expensive media channels they don't need. And, believe me, outdoor advertising is expensive. Actually, the problem is broader than that. Most people think a Marketer's job is to sell the public lots of expensive things they don't need. This was brought home to me recently at Harare airport, where the Immigration Officer read my occupation and sniffed, 'So, you sell the people what they don't need?' (This from an official of the Mugabe regime!)

Outdoor advertising, used sensibly and creatively, is a powerful reminder medium. This means that you should never use it on its own, but only in tandem with radio or TV advertising to reinforce the main message of your campaign. This reminder medium has well-established creative guidelines, key amongst them is the injunction not to say too much.

But, what concerns me more is the sheer volume of outdoor advertising that blights Africa. My friends at Synovate tell me there are in fact 9,443 outdoor impressions in Kenya. 20% of these are whopping great billboards, and a surprising 65% streetlight boxes. Nairobi has 56% of all such signage, with the next most affected areas being Nyanza and Coast, each with 11%. If you want to get away from billboards altogether, move to Central Region (2%) where you can still see the wood for the trees.

Once the next Kenya National Census has reported, we will all be able to see whether these concentrations of high visibility advertising sites make any commercial sense. But even if the weighting has a logic, the volume doesn't. The biggest advertisers on outdoor are mobile phone companies and banks. They use acres of vinyl to tell us how big they are, how much better life is with them around, and how committed they are to us. So much visibility, for so little sincerity!

First published July 2001

▶ Creativity Tip 4 – mind your language

We live and work in a region that uses language well. East Africans are not, by nature, very profane people. Cursing in the workplace is frowned upon. Western expatriates are often surprised to discover that swearing at staff doesn't work here; it shuts internal communication down.

Our Advertising Standards apparatus is rarely challenged on matters of taste. So, when something vulgar appears in the public domain, it stands out more than it would on any other Continent. Currently the insurance company GA is having a general accident with its latest billboard campaign.

In one execution, a photograph shows a man walking along using his mobile phone and about to fall down an open manhole. The headline exclaims: 'S**t Happens!' The intended takeout from the ad seems to be that if 'S**t Happens' to you, you'll be fine so long as you have paid your premium to GA. I have several issues with this.

Firstly, what kind of brand swears to attract your attention? What would you say about a person who behaved in this way? Maybe I should loosen up, because it's 'only advertising' and the brand is 'just having fun'. But if this is a deliberate piece of brand communication, someone at GA must have written the brief 'make the tone vulgar; have a bit of a laugh.'

Secondly, the man in the ad deserves to fall down a manhole, because he is walking along texting and not looking where he is going. So, what is GA telling this careless person? It's OK to be irresponsible because that's what insurance is here for: to pay medical and repair bills incurred by irresponsible people? Few Insurance Actuaries would agree with this, as writing insurance involves a careful calculation of the risk and the attendant cover required. A major element is likely policyholder behaviour.

Thirdly, what is the GA brand promising about its claims resolution? The ad seems to say that even an idiot can fall down a manhole and enjoy speedy claim settlement. That doesn't tally with most people's experience of insurance.

GA is right: S**t does indeed happen. But few brands would choose to let it happen on their own billboards.

First published June 2018

▶ Creativity Tip 5 – be media neutral

There comes a point in every Marketing conversation when the client decides they need some advertising. Sometimes this comes early in the conversation; sometimes it's the first thing they say. But usually they are not mandating advertising as a solution, they are simply saying they need to get their message out there.

And that's fine. But when someone really does mean 'we need some advertising' they tend to be a junior person whose boss has told them that advertising is what they want. Few Marketers in this position pause to question that instruction. They move straight into execution, as if their jobs depended upon it. Which is a pity, because a little quiet consideration at this point can often save a great deal of disappointment later on. Better than that, it can set the conditions for something even more powerful than advertising to be created.

When a business needs to say something important to the market, it's generally a good idea to begin without too many preconceptions. Don't place constraints on the form or content of the Marketing communication at this early stage of the process. Instead, start your planning with a 'media neutral' attitude.

A good way to start the process is to gather together two or three of the clearest thinkers in your business (not necessarily Marketers). Season this group with a couple of outside experts – perhaps a smart PR person or a senior advertising creative person. Then host a series of short sessions where you try to develop the strongest promise your brand can make in the forthcoming campaign. Consider the target audience you must persuade if your campaign is to work, and be ruthless about stripping away audiences that are not critical. Check your intended messaging against what the competition is saying. Finally, consider all the ways in which you could reach them, and prioritise those channels. If well-facilitated, this can be a stimulating and enjoyable session that produces some surprising outcomes.

In 2002, Toyota launched the latest model of Corolla in the UK. The Corolla is a good car, but as a brand it is anodyne. It works, it looks OK and... that's it. So, the Toyota team had to find an emotional hook to hang the campaign upon. They settled on 'Corolla. A car to be proud of'.

Instead of mandating conventional media choices, they launched their campaign with a stunt: printing and distributing free vinyl car covers with the new Corolla printed on them. This gave motorists the chance to 'cover up' their existing car with a new Corolla, and jokingly pretend they owned one themselves.

Then Toyota placed volunteers in crowds at televised football matches, who would stand up whenever a goal was scored holding banners proclaiming 'I've got a new Corolla!'

In TV and on radio they developed hundreds of stories about people going to extraordinary lengths to be associated with the new Corolla. And so, impact was created and demand generated. Will your next 'advertising' campaign be half as brilliant?

First published October 2016

Let's meet a
Creative Champion

Judy Kibinge

Judy Kibinge is a Kenyan filmmaker and founding Director of Docubox, East Africa's first Documentary Film Fund. She also happens to be a member of the Academy of Motion Picture Arts and Sciences, and serves on The Academy's Documentary Committee.

In 1992, Judy joined McCann Erickson, then East Africa's largest advertising agency. She rose to be the first non-expatriate and female Creative Director of an international agency in the region. Judy spent the 1990's creating award-winning ads for big brands. Most famously, 'Tusker. My Country. My Beer.'

She quit to become a self-taught filmmaker in 2000. Her first feature film 'Dangerous Affair' (2002) was set in the heart of middle class Nairobi and is widely believed to have kicked off the wave of contemporary filmmaking in Kenya. Her third dramatic feature 'Something Necessary' premiered at TIFF (Toronto) in 2013. In 2013, she founded the first independently created documentary film fund on the continent, Docubox.

Over the past six years, the fund has supported over 20 feature documentaries and offered training workshops and screenings to thousands more. Docubox held the first Sub-Saharan Good Pitch in October 2018, an extraordinary day where 267 individuals from 13 countries and 161 organizations came to lend their support to six powerful films, tackling some of the most important social and environmental issues of our time. In 2018, she was selected to be a Sundance Fellow, as part of a global project to tell stories of change.

Talking of the importance of creativity in general, Judy says: 'Creativity is how mankind advances itself. Creators are able to transcend traditional viewpoints and envision the world in new ways, uniquely connecting new thoughts and ideas through their imagination. For our continent to truly become great, we need to acknowledge the power of creativity and offer creative thinkers the support needed to both imagine a brave new future and also encourage self-reflection. Thereby empowering humanity to be more than it presently is.'

Chapter 7

Public Profile

The practise of Public and Media Relations in East Africa has recently become very much more professional. Twenty years ago, PR was used by big companies for damage limitation and crisis management. Fixing the media and killing stories. Handling the airline crash, the packaging failure, contaminated food or disappointing Annual Results.

As bigger corporations emerged, governance improved. Stock Exchanges were created and institutional reputations required more proactive management. A new generation of PR men and women rose to prominence, with better professional qualifications and wider sectoral experience. Most Advertising Agencies sprouted PR departments which evolved into well-known professional service brands. There were strong independent PR Agencies too. Over time, the biggest sought affiliation with global PR brands.

Nowadays the making and breaking of reputations can happen very quickly in online channels. Consumers have found their voice in social media. Media coverage of mistakes or malfeasance can no longer be muzzled. Public Relations is now a hearts and minds exercise; and successful Media Relations requires the building of trust over the long term.

On the client side, we have more professional Corporate Affairs teams. But, in my view at least, the understanding of how to build positive profile for brands still lags behind that of corporate PR.

The evolution of Public Relations

It's not often you get to hear from one of the greats. But the other day I had the opportunity to listen to an interview with Harold Burson, co-founder of global Public Relations practice Burson-Marsteller. He's a quintessential 1960's PR practitioner, still active at age 91. Americans aren't drawn to the concept of a peaceful retirement. Mr. Burson comes from the generation who built big brands and drove great political initiatives in the U.S. He also understood that PR on its own was less effective than

PR combined with work in other channels. So, he was one of the first to collaborate with an Advertising Agency, and later sold his business to one.

In the interview, he answered a question that is pertinent to the practice of Public Relations in Africa today. *Do you think the role of PR is still misunderstood?*

This is what he said in reply: 'If you took a census of people in PR the definition would centre around communications. I maintain that PR has two components: to help devise policies and procedures that are acceptable to the people you want to reach and when you communicate these effectively, you will succeed. So, the PR function covers a much broader spectrum than just getting out news releases. You have to operate in the public interest, and PR has a role to play in the reconciliation of what the public wants and the client expects. Unlike in the political sphere, where you can make claims and not be held accountable, corporations can't do that. The more sophisticated companies understand this. The Chinese are doing more to build a quality image for their products. Japan moved from the cheap end to the top end. The thinking has been: 'if we make the cheapest products, people will buy them', but the public is much more sophisticated than that.'

Mr. Burson went on to discuss the importance of good Public Relations to any major enterprise. He is adamant that the CEO should be the person who represents the corporation publicly. There should be close contact between the CEO and the chief PR officer. They must identify closely with one another. If there is a change in CEO, there is usually a requirement for a new chief PR officer because the CEO needs a personal adviser and interpreter.

This speaks against established habits in Africa. Here, we find PR Managers in big companies who outlast several CEOs. And sometimes PR practitioners who become bigger media personalities than their clients!

Drawn to talk about PR's impact on business, Mr. Burson had this to say: 'In more sophisticated markets, we are being evaluated on outcome. Whether it be promoting a product or assisting a company in legislation. A lot more research is being done into outcomes. You can only measure if you have really good research. In the past, companies didn't spend as much as they should on measurement, but that is changing.'

This is an area where Africa needs to get in step with the rest of the world, after a worrying decade where investment in Market

Research has been choked off. More and more Companies are now refreshing their understanding of their markets.

In closing, Mr. Burson said this about the kind of people the PR industry needs in the future: 'I have a lot of optimism about the role of PR as a business tool and I think PR people increasingly have a better understanding of business. Those in charge of hiring are insisting that people know more about the businesses they serve. That they understand how a sale is made, and what can go wrong. Much more is demanded in terms of quality from candidates for top communications jobs. Ten years from now, having an MBA may be a base requirement for getting the top job in communications. What we're looking for now are people with skills in specific environments. For example, people who can mix experience in NGOs with PR practise. We're also hiring people such as lawyers who do not want to practice law, or people who have had experience with regulatory agencies in healthcare. In tech, we look for people who know what's inside that black box, not just what it does. It's a matter of being able to understand what the different priorities are in different sectors.'

Broader based knowledge within the PR industry certainly makes good business sense for Africa.

First published April 2014

Manage that reputation

As a general statement, I am not in favour of acronyms. In my experience, they are a barrier to understanding. Experts use acronyms to maintain their superiority. Bluffers use acronyms for the same reason. Company managers sometimes shortens the name of their enterprise to reduce time in meetings and on emails. Within a few months a business goes from being the Delicious Sausage Company to DSC. Within a year DSC becomes the name of the organisation... and the employees soon forget that they are in the business of producing delicious sausages.

CSR is an acronym that merits investigation. Not least because the activity it signals is no longer as clearly understood as it once was. It actually came into use in the 1960's as a form of self-regulation built into modern business models, and ISO 26000 is its international standard. But today, opinion is divided between people who believe that CSR is a distraction from the hard-nosed strategies that drive successful business, and those who think it is flagrant window dressing.

For businesses that run the risk of attracting public criticism, Corporate Social Responsibility can be a useful tool in rebalancing public opinion. For that reason, sectors like Oil and Gas, Pharmaceuticals and Alcoholic Beverages have the greatest enthusiasm for CSR. For example, just before the Marketing of tobacco brands became all but untenable in the West, fag factories started running campaigns in the developing world aimed at preventing young people from taking up smoking. These were largely rubbished by the anti-smoking lobby.

Business people should do what they can to offset risks to corporate reputations. If their business involves drilling for oil several kilometres beneath a polar bear's nest, then it's prudent to pledge passionate support for alternative energy. If their dividend yield relies on developing then controlling the supply of a desperately needed medicine, it might make sense to take the lead in an orphan drug project.

Before you jump to the conclusion that this sector is doing dreadful things to orphans, I should explain that an orphan drug is a cure for a condition that only affects a small percentage of the population. It is therefore deemed economically unattractive, so no one wants to own it. How consumers feel about this kind of CSR rather depends upon their own moral compass. For some cynics, the acronym signals Conscience Salving Remedy!

Marketing textbooks reveal that CSR is about 'operating a business in a manner that accounts for the social and environmental impact it creates'. CSR is intended to aid an organisation's mission as well as provide a guide to what the company stands for. And you won't be surprised to hear me say that CSR strategy should be derived from Brand strategy. Or that it should be both future-focused and creative. If your brand is about tasty coffee, carefully grown with due respect to environment and growers, it's not hard to see where you should be investing in CSR.

However, you encounter a problem in the event that your brand is not properly defined. If its values are worthwhile yet generic. If its mission statement is a catch-all cornucopia; and its promise to the market has no competitive edge. Spot those brands every week in newspaper pictorials. They donate bicycles and wheelchairs to grateful, yet puzzled, recipients. There's plainly no connection between this activity and the promise of their brand.

First published March 2016

Take care of your personal branding

There's a good deal of talk these days about personal branding. Here in East Africa we have experts running events and offering personal consultations to aspirant and established leaders alike. It's a growing market, powered by an increasing awareness that it really does matter what other people think and feel about you. This is a good thing. Only a decade ago the prevailing attitude among leaders was that they could do and say what they wanted, and if people didn't like it they could lump it.

The social media explosion has helped accelerate the shift. Say the right thing or put a foot wrong: either way you can instantly feature on thousands of small screens.

Getting personal branding right can become a career in its own right. Over in the United States a wealthy yet surprisingly unsuccessful businessman with an awkward personal manner is in the running to be the next President. His personal brand just happens to resonate with a huge number of his disaffected countrymen and women. In the UK, a retired footballer, his former pop singer wife and their children are all working to create one of the most valuable brands in the western world. Brand Beckham is currently estimated to be worth half a billion Sterling Pounds (US$771m). The brand is used to add value to the family's ventures in a multitude of sectors. Researchers at The London School of Marketing estimate that Brand Beckham generates between £30 and £40 million per year. The Beckham brand power resides in the family's three main corporate vehicles. Footworks, under which David's football-related revenues are collated. The Beckham label, for all their brand endorsements. And Beckham Venture, for Victoria's fashion business.

Interestingly, researchers found that the Beckham label has grown in value more rapidly since David, 40, gave up his professional football career. As David and Victoria have focused more on their respective businesses, both have seen increases in profitability. Beckham Ventures could achieve a three times multiple on turnover this year compared to last. The opening of Victoria's flagship clothing store in London last year and the positive response to her New York Fashion Week show prove how she has shifted from 90's pop star to established fashion designer.

Whilst Victoria keeps busy with her booming fashion brand, David recently partnered with beverage giant Diageo to launch

Scotch whisky brand, Haig Club. He recently celebrated ten years of fragrances, has his own range with H&M and models for Belstaff.

And it's not just the parents who are making waves in the media. Their eldest son Brooklyn has also caught the media's eye. In his first interview with the international magazine Miss Vogue, Brooklyn discussed how he's gained over four million followers on Instagram and shared his top tips with readers. Last year, younger brother Romeo fronted the Christmas advertising campaign for fashion powerhouse Burberry, who claim he helped boost their sales by 14 per cent.

Anton Dominique, the Chief Marketing Officer at the London School of Marketing, says: 'The Beckham brand has been used to advertise everything from designer clothes to satellite television and even whisky. What is also interesting is that the family name is almost as influential as any individual family member. The Beckham name has the Midas touch when it comes to advertising, and the mere mention of the name being associated with a brand is a news event in itself.'

The famous family is richer than the Queen of England, and ranks second only to her own family in terms of brand recognition. After the Royals, the Beckhams are Britain's most recognisable family with a global pulling power that's almost second to none. Personal branding as a family business – will this be a development in our own regional economy?

First published July 2016

Beware the advertising supplement

If you are a CEO, a Marketing Director or a Brand Manager you probably suffer from a periodic affliction. It comes upon you in the middle of a busy working day, causes irritation and is very hard to treat. The symptoms present in the form of repeated phone calls from a newspaper sales representative you do not know, sounding more familiar that she should. This often leads to mild anxiety, when she tells you that your brand will be eclipsed by its competitors if you do not agree to taking an advertising supplement.

The supplement is an anachronism. It is a way of trying to flog space that's practised by newspaper Sales Reps who have never made the effort to create anything new. They have targets to make, and they are operating in a category that PR friend of mine calls Legacy Media because it's on the way out. So, the idea of an advertising supplement is usually born on a slow Friday, in an exchange between two Sales Reps that goes something like this. Rep 1: 'Shoes. They seem to be popular these days.' Rep 2: 'Great idea! Let's call anyone who has feet.'

I should tell you that newspaper editorial teams loathe having to write industry supplements. So, they put the lowest possible level of talent on the job. The Picture Desk is prevailed upon to find suitable images from the stack of unused pics sent in by PR agencies. Normally the kind of un-caption-able images that end up with the caption:

'Hello! Minister greets Harris Christopher, MD of The Inside Brand at his Nairobi premises.'

Then a Sub-Editor is diverted from her main interest: writing an unprintable first novel. The Designer with the thickest spectacles and thinnest understanding of typeface is enlisted to design the layout. Perhaps a tea lady is co-opted for her surprising insights on footwear. And, hey presto, we're good to go. So, the sales team now turns its attention to blackmailing your suppliers and business partners to place supporting ads to bulk out the supplement. These come in a time-honoured format employed by people who resent the obligation: 'Mbuzi Technology is proud to support The Bank of Bujumbura.' They have absolutely no commercial impact.

Advertising supplements could conceivably offer value, but only if the approach is overhauled. If there was any consideration of a target audience, and what they might be interested in reading. If the editorial team was interested in transforming perceptions of a business sector. If design and layout aimed to show participating brands in the best possible light and evoke the spirit of the sector being profiled. If a respected industry commentator was recruited to open the supplement with a stimulating opinion piece.

Until that time, my advice is to say 'no' just as quickly as you can.

First published January 2015

Here are five tips on creating a better profile for your brand.

▶ Profiling Tip 1 – share the good news

Sometimes you are so busy that you lose perspective. When this happens to companies, they lose market perspective. Their senior Production people have installed a line that will double output and enable them to offer a new form of packaging to the market. Their

Distribution guys have taken two years to rework depot structure and trunking schedules so that customers in Mbarara can receive goods ex-Mombasa 12 hours earlier. Their IT team has redesigned the website user experience to ensure that visitors get to their intended destination in no more than 3 clicks. But, after all this effort, the market has simply not noticed any change.

I have sat in many meetings where senior business people have expressed that they're frustrated with the market. 'What do we have to do for the market to acknowledge our hard work?' The answer is very simple: 'Tell them'.

I recall an African security business with a track record of thirty years of practical innovation. They had pioneered manned guarding, then alarm response, dog patrols and even electric buttons placed at intervals around a compound for the askari to press on his perambulations and thus record his progress. They were branded Securicor, but when I met them they were outraged that their brand name had become a generic: 'People in this market even ask each other what kind of Securicor they have got!'

The commercial outcome was predictable: Securicor failed to command the price that the brand merited.

The problem was this: they had never reported all this progress in a meaningful and memorable way. Not through PR which, when well written and photographed, is almost free. And certainly not through advertising. In fact, they came from the school of thought that asks 'why would we need advertising?' They had thousands of guards in training and on deployment and the biggest market share of security contracts – but this blinded them to a simple truth. That the market is not obliged to see things your way. To put together branded vehicles, signs on people's gates, and smart uniforms into a holistic appreciation of your offering.

The Marketer's responsibility is to make their Brand Promise clear to the market and be tireless in demonstrating on-brand delivery. I know huge poultry businesses who have done remarkable things to breed chickens humanely, hygienically and profitably. If I told you how many chicks they breed every week you would whistle. I know microfinance businesses that transact millions of dollars in tiny loans every month without mishap. I know people who can triple the yield of the small potato farmer, so that when he pulls up his plant at harvest time he dances around the field waving enlarged tubers in gay abandon. But if I told you their brand names, you would not play back these amazing facts to me. These nuggets of excellence. Your perceptions would date from the last time you interacted with them, and that might have been decades ago. Or never.

It's a heartening fact that so many successful businesses in Africa are moving into their third, fifth and even eighth decade of operation. That is something to celebrate. Not just at the Christmas party or the AGM, but in regular dialogue with the marketplace. And now that we have online channels there really is no excuse. It is time to communicate your evolving brand narrative.

First published July 2012

▶ Profiling Tip 2 – first impressions still count

Your grandmother always told you that first impressions count, and she was a wise old bird. She knew that smart, well-polished, shoes were the first priority for men. Modest yet modish dress and subtle makeup for women. A firm handshake and good eye contact for both.

When it comes to your personal brand, you need to give first impressions proper consideration. So that you can make a consistently positive impact each and every time. Here's some interesting new research on business wear. It comes from California State University, and is a study called The Cognitive Consequences of Formal Clothing. Surprisingly, from a State that espouses informality, this study suggests that wearing smart clothes changes the way we think.

It reveals that dressing well makes you feel happier in yourself, and more powerful in a group. This is a good thing, because when you feel powerful you are more capable of abstract thinking. Abstraction is a mark of civilized development, and allows thinkers to break conceptual bounds.

Here's another insight: well-dressed people feel emotionally removed from others. Professor Abraham Rutchik says: 'We feel less compassion, and perceive the emotions of others less.'

Dressing for success means different things at different times. Only the scaliest old reptile buttons himself into a big double-breasted suit for every occasion. But one of the hardest things to do is to know how casual to make things. There's now a growing acceptance that 'dressing down' for work does not work. The key is to think about some words that you can use (to yourself) to define your brand personality. As with commercial brands, the simpler and more interesting these words are, the better. Edgy wins hands down over innovative. Robust is easier to understand than confident. Witty is more focused than sociable.

First impressions require more thought when you are a senior person representing your organisational brand. You have to sit down and cross-reference those descriptive words. The Administrator of a big hospital with excellent community engagement might need to look softer and more caring than the CEO of a modern airline, who might exude a mix of technical competence and stylish hospitality. But these are only nuances. If you are a large, forthright lady, you may not feel comfortable portraying yourself as fluffy. So, don't force it. If you don't to live comfortably within your brand identity, you won't be able to maintain it.

There is no question that modern African society is investing more in looking sharp. We're enjoying it too. And giving new inspiration to tailors, dressmakers and fashion designers. Ten years ago, our cities were full of small tailoring operations producing garments commissioned in hope but worn with regret. From the Kaunda Suit to the bodyguard jacket, our clothing was as horrible as our architecture. But in the second decade of a new century we have almost endless opportunities to style up. From mitumba to Hugo Boss, Manolo Blahnik to Bata – what will your personal brand wear tomorrow?

First published June 2016

▶ Profiling Tip 3 – always bounce back

When you make products, they sometimes fail. If they are brands, that failure can quickly damage equity. The breakfast cereal that is stale. The batteries that are duds. The car that is unsafe.

Here's a surprising story from the world of technology. It concerns Apple, a brand I use and love. A brand I associate with humanity and innovation; whose retail stores are an example to more traditional businesses and whose staff give the impression that they'll happily do what it takes to make you satisfied. But when it came to product failures, Apple's traditional crisis management stance was to stonewall as long as possible. To make no comment until market pressure forced an abject apology.

Until an incident in Apple's burgeoning Chinese business forced an more savvy approach. Last month, a Chinese lady was electrocuted to death by a (probably) fake iPhone charger. A similar incident the following week put a gentleman in a coma. The Apple team swung into action and launched a buyback programme for fake iPhone chargers that is little short of brilliant.

Apple offered a charger amnesty. Its retail outlets will take back any iPhone, iPod, or iPad chargers not made by Apple and in exchange will sell users an authentic Apple USB power adaptor for $10 – half the usual price. Customers have to bring in their Apple gadgets, each of which has a unique serial number, and are limited to one discounted charger per device. Commentator Chen Yifei lauded this as a genius move: 'In a single stroke, Apple has inoculated itself from blame if any further third-party chargers disastrously melt down and fail. If it had chosen to do nothing, it might eventually have had to face some uncomfortable questions about overpriced chargers.'

Even at 50% off, Apple may still be making a profit on the chargers. And let's not forget that Apple's take-back programme will generate a surge of extra foot traffic to Apple Stores, where users trading in their chargers may well decide on impulse to buy another Apple product. Apple user Sina Weibo blogged: 'Apple is calculating. The programme saves its reputation on one hand, it also generates profit.'

The newer, smarter Apple crisis management strategy may be a reflection of the fact that Apple, while still very profitable, understands it can no longer be the impervious, non-responsive tech titan it once was. What lessons can we learn from this for Marketing in Africa? Probably the simplest take-out is that when failure happens, you give the customer a pleasant surprise. A happily surprised customer is more likely to be a loyal customer.

First published May 2017

▶ Profiling Tip 4 – use great images

It's been a funny old week. On Monday, I was run off the road by a huge slice of motorised pizza. Full marks for impact, Pizza Inn, but none for brand engagement.

Then yesterday I was at a photocall. The subject was very interesting. We were planning to announce a new partnership with WWF. A bevy of PR people fluttered around us, ostensibly directing the best PR photo we could create. But the directions given included 'Can you just smile at each other?' and 'Please point at the logo'. This is how Africa produces some of the worst PR photographs on the planet.

My rough estimate is that PR agencies influence less than 20% of newspaper picture content in Africa. This is low by global standards. But the greater sadness is that the PR-directed content is no more creative than standard Picture Desk imagery. PR pictures should add life, impact and colour to any newspaper, magazine, blog or website. So, what makes a good PR photograph?

- It has to bring together the most important elements of a story into a single image that makes the audience interested in knowing more.
- It must dramatise the story through its choice of locations, casting, wardrobe and props.
- If it features a brand, that brand should be central to the image.
- The image needs to be technically perfect. Properly lit and framed. With the protagonists shown in a positive light – not in mid-speech, with their eyes half closed.
- Both the image and its caption should fit the editorial tone of the publication for which it is intended.

There is a generally-held belief about how PR photography should be done, that is conservative and wrong. Few Marketing people really understand this PR value equation: higher production values + interesting set up = greater impact.

Nowadays, the most interesting pictures in any newspaper are to be found at the back, and I don't mean on the sports pages. Must you really be Promoted to Glory before you get a decent PR picture?

First published August 2011

▶ Profiling Tip 5 – Take care online

CEOs are increasingly being drawn into social media conversations. Sometimes unwittingly, when their personal social media impacts their business reputation. Sometimes deliberately, as part of personal brand building or corporate communication.

Back in 2015 the CEO of US tech company Hootsuite shared an Instagram image of his hand holding a festive drink with the caption 'Cheers to my Homies!' But the company had just completed a restructuring exercise and made 65 people redundant. The subsequent social media storm featured comments like: 'I bet that tastes sweet, now that the dirty work is done'.

So, it's worth taking the time to decide on your personal social media identity, and separate your business and personal accounts. The most attractive public personae come across as very human. Sir Richard Branson strives to reply personally and often adds personal comments and pictures. Asked how much time he devotes to this he says, 'I make sure to check in at least a couple of times a day.'

It helps if you invest in a platform that enables you to consolidate what's happening on all social media accounts. This allows for closer management and make cross-posting much easier. While many of us are juggling Twitter, LinkedIn and Facebook, we should also consider visual channels like Instagram and You Tube to highlight company events. East African battery and solar company Chloride Exide last year posted staff performing an impromptu song and dance, and received ten times more interest than their previous posts and memes had ever generated. Evidence of team spirit and happy culture resonate well with consumers.

As a CEO, your messaging should point readers and viewers in the right direction. Ideally by posting links to the relevant part of your company website or blog. Driving traffic towards your team, who should be briefed and equipped to handle it. Building traffic, interest and potential leads for the business will also help you to rationalise the time you spend being active on social media.

According to Forbes magazine, most Fortune 500 CEOs don't use social media. Many say they are too busy, others fear opprobrium, and still more reject the idea that their messaging can be created for them by others. For some leaders, sharing their corporate direction with a broader public seems treasonable. And to be fair, many CEO agendas aren't interesting enough to share. As with most aspects of CEO life, this is all about control or the loss of it. But when almost all your customers, partners, staff and competitors are active online, surely avoidance is the wrong strategy.

My own recommendation is to practice scarcity. To appear from time to time, when you have something interesting to say.

First published January 2014

Let's meet a
Profiling Professional

Joe Otin

Joe Otin is the CEO of the interactive Ad Agency, The Collective, and has 25 years' experience of profile building in advertising, online content production, media and Market Research. He is the chairman of the Advertising Standards Board in Kenya, a past president of the Pan-African Media Research Organisation and a member of the oversight committee of Kenya Audience Research Foundation.

Joe is an active Rotarian, and currently the District Governor Elect responsible for Rotary Clubs in Kenya, Ethiopia, Eritrea and South Sudan. He is the Rotary International representative to UN Environment, and a past member of the Rotary International Membership and Communications Committees. He has presided as the chief judge of the Public Relations Society of Kenya Excellence Awards, having served on the panel for 11 years, and was the chief judge of the Marketing Society of Kenya gala awards in 2015.

He himself was granted the MSK Marketing Warrior Award in 2010, and has published several papers at local and international conferences, most recently on return-on-investment in advertising and social media. Joe has served as a judge for the Top 40 Under 40 Women and the Top 40 Under 40 Men in Kenya. He is also a Marketing columnist for the Business Daily.

On using PR to build profile, Joe says: 'I like to think of PR as good behaviour that is told in an interesting story, and there are three things that really matter when it comes to driving a positive image. Firstly, you should start with a strong sense of purpose and clearly define the overall goal. Secondly, have a good understanding of your audience and spend time listening to them. Finally, deliver a consistent message that is based on your goals and relevant to the people that mean the most to you, because consistency builds trust.'

Chapter 8

Brand Delivery

In this, the closing chapter, I wanted to open a window on the latest stage of my working life. After more than thirty years of creating and promoting brands – and communicating their promises to the market – I now work inside organisations to reshape their cultures. The two are inextricably connected. Most brands and businesses fail to achieve optimal results because of a lack of alignment. Cultural norms and employee behaviours are not in line with promises made to customers. This results in various levels of customer disappointment, which in turn impact brand loyalty, repeat sales and recommendation.

They are also connected in methodology and approach. The techniques that Marketers use to persuade external audiences can also be applied to internal audiences. In particular, the insights and creativity required to produce real impact on consumers are just as necessary when planning employee communications. Understanding the nuances of humanity is common to both.

Organisational change, or Culture Transformation as we like to call it, is relatively new to Africa. The early proponents were the management consultancy teams in the major audit firms. Understandably their focus was on cost and structural efficiencies, not human beings.

My new focus is on releasing human potential inside branded businesses. Opening up new possibilities by engaging employees as people and tapping into their ideas and energy. The impact of this is primarily commercial, and we measure it at customer touchpoints. We look for improvements in Customer Effort and Net Promoter Scores, customer loyalty and repurchase patterns. Of course, we are also interested in happier, more productive employees who enjoy their work and are recognised for their contribution. Altogether, it is fascinating and rewarding work. And, who knows, maybe there'll be another book in it!

Exemplary brand delivery

Last week I co-hosted a breakfast forum on building stronger business cultures in Nairobi. We hope to repeat the exercise in Kampala and Dar in due course. It was a great session, because the CEOs and HR leaders who joined us were genuinely interested in the issue. And, specifically, in how you shape a company culture to deliver your Brand Promise.

But the highlight for me was hearing a keynote speaker who has actually practised what we were preaching. First in the Public Sector, then in Barclays Bank, Kenya Airways and more recently the regional brewing giant East African Breweries. Three powerful corporate brands that impact the lives of millions of East Africans daily.

Paul Kasimu is well placed to be one of our future lions of industry. He's a Human Resources professional with an intuitive understanding of brands. So far in the history of Africa's economic growth, neither specialisation has yet produced many company leaders. Most of those roles still go to financial or operational people. Which is a pity, because many of our enterprises have grown beyond getting the processes and numbers right.

To move off the current plateau, we need leaders who understand that brand must be the most motivating summary of your commercial reason for being. And understand that African employees are ready to respond enthusiastically to any alternative to traditional, hierarchical leadership styles. Paul spoke for about ten minutes. He captured the attention of the room, and I'd like to share the insights he revealed. Firstly, he talked about the concept of High Performing Organisations. Using examples from his experience he defined these as places where:

- There is leadership at all levels with the courage, energy and capability to deliver on ambitious performance goals
- Roles and responsibilities are clear to all
- The best talent is deployed in the right places
- A customer service ethos is institutionalised, and staff behaviours are instinctive
- Differential rewards are aligned to employee performance

On the subject of rewards, Paul is very much in favour of employee performance being measured against organisational values – the values of the corporate brand. When you are part of a culture as public as an airline, you very quickly get to know whether staff are aligned to the brand. And Paul shared with us something that every senior airline manager has experienced – the privilege of being phoned at home in the middle of the night by someone who has not enjoyed their brand experience!

Paul went on to talk about the importance of building an envied Employer Brand. In simple terms, the kind of Company that people would love to work for. For their own development and reputation – not for opportunities to supplement their salaries with shady side deals. He talked about the uncomfortable business of having to let employees go. Something even the most successful businesses find themselves doing, because in the private sector we are no longer about providing jobs for life. In fact, Paul has a stronger concept: we should be in the business of creating employability for life. Having business cultures that identify, develop and promote talent in individuals to the extent that their future is assured, even if they are no longer working for you.

Building great company cultures should be rewarding for everyone in the organisation. It is actually impossible to impose cultural norms on human beings without giving them some form of ownership. Ownership of both the rational and the emotional dimensions. The 'what we do' coupled with 'this is how we do it'. These days, most of us expect to work in many different enterprises during our careers. Generally, we aspire to work in organisations where the brand is liked; the behaviours admirable and the customers satisfied. When we move on, we try to take with us the best of what we experienced.

But wouldn't it also be an achievement to build a culture that people could leave, and then return to later in life's journey? Coming back to add even more value, drawn from broader experience and fresher perspectives. One measure of a really strong business culture is this: good people who leave later aspire to return, and are welcomed back with open arms.

First published February 2015

Selling your brand inside your Company

When you think about Marketing, you more than likely think of Marketing to your customers; persuading more people to buy what you sell. But there's another audience that is just as important: your employees. The people who can make the brand come alive for your customers, and deliver the commercial returns you seek.

But, in my experience, many companies either ignore this critical constituency or pay lip service to it.

Internal Marketing and communication is very important. Done well, it's the best way to create a powerful emotional connection between the employee and the products and services you sell. Without that connection, employees are likely to undermine the expectations set by your advertising. In some cases, because they simply don't understand what you have promised the public. In others, because they don't actually believe in the brand and they feel disengaged from the company. By contrast, when people care about and believe in the brand, they're motivated to work harder and their loyalty to the company increases.

While most executives recognise the need to keep people informed about the company's strategy and direction, few understand the need to persuade employees. What's more, the HR professionals charged with internal communication don't actually have the Marketing skills to communicate successfully. Information is doled out to employees in the form of traditional memos, newsletters and bulletins. The Marketing Department might get involved once in a while to tell employees about a new ad campaign. But, usually, the intent is to tell people what the company is doing (information), not to sell them on the big ideas (persuasion).

I have found that by applying the principles of consumer advertising to internal communications, leaders can guide employees to a better understanding of, and passion for, the brand vision. This enables employees to 'live' the vision in their daily work. And when employees live the vision, customers are more likely to experience what you've promised them.

But it's critical to choose the right moment. Most employees have limited tolerance for change initiatives – rebranding or visioning exercises are no exception. But at certain turning points, when the company is experiencing some fundamental challenge or change, employees seek direction and become relatively receptive to these kinds of initiatives. Such moments can generate either positive or negative energy; enthusiasm for new directions or unproductive rumour-mongering. So, they must be seized, and used to shape a deliberate outcome.

British Petroleum seized such an opportunity when it merged with Amoco and then ARCO. It rebranded itself as BP, redesigned its logo, and launched a campaign simultaneously to staff and the public declaring that it was going 'beyond petroleum'. The company put aside its identity as an oil company to become an energy company, and took the opportunity to move from an old-style, closed corporation to a modern, collaborative, new-economic venture. This break with the past gave employees from each of the original companies a new and distinctive identity. A survey that was taken after the internal re-branding campaign showed that 76% of employees felt favourably toward the new brand, 80% were aware of the values in the new brand messages, and 90% thought the company was going in the right direction.

The arrival of a new leader is a highly opportune moment for internal redirection. Staff expect to hear from a new leader right away, and are usually open to new ideas at such times. Carly Fiorina exploited this window when she took over Hewlett-Packard. She took a personal interest in the branding strategy and played a public and active role. To demonstrate her commitment, Fiorina appeared in launch commercials, which asserted that, 'the original start-up, will act like one again'. The Company's new tagline 'HP Invent' became a mantra, and co-founder Bill Hewlett's garage, where he and Dave Packard made their first inventions, became an icon that featured both in internal and external communications. In this way, a new leader repurposed the company's original heritage to release a surge of employee energy.

First published February 2017

Taking your people on a journey

The other day I found myself in a strange place. I was upstairs in one of Kenya's biggest supermarkets, looking at my fellow shoppers on CCTV. I was there because, as I was shortly to discover, I had been robbed. I had popped in to the store with a brown envelope of petty cash to buy some office stationery, and it had disappeared.

When I reported my loss, Nakumatt staff were both concerned and helpful. Within minutes I was watching a video history of the previous 20 minutes of life in the store. It was a bit like having an out-of-body experience. I was actually quite excited as I waited to solve the mystery of the missing envelope.

There on screen is the stationery aisle and, moments later, here I come. Up and down I go. I locate the orange folders I have been looking for. I pull the brown envelope out of my back pocket to check my shopping list and I gather up an armful of the folders. And in doing so, I drop the envelope. There it lies in plain view in the middle of the aisle as I walk out of shot. Twelve different customers transit the aisle. Most don't even see the envelope lying there. One lady pushes her trolley around it.

And then it happens. A well-dressed lady walks down the aisle behind me. She sees the envelope, stoops and picks it up. She has clearly seen the cash. She half turns and looks at me for a split second. Then she makes her decision, turns quickly and walks away with my money.

The Nakumatt man with the CCTV looks at me and shrugs: put that one down to experience. But I'll do better than that, because the episode gives me an excellent analogy for the way people react to changes in company culture.

Put aside the rejecters: they rarely remain a problem for long. In the context of a well-run change programme they soon isolate themselves and either depart or become obvious targets for replacement. More interesting are employees who might be predisposed to culture change. They demonstrate up to six shades of reaction:

- Attention
- Awareness
- Acceptance
- Advocacy
- Action
- Adherence.

The test of a good change programme is whether it can move staff from Attention to Adherence. To do this, it should engage employees in four ways:

- Hearing – receiving the right messages through relevant channels, in the correct tone of voice
- Head – considering the logical benefits of culture change for the business, and for themselves
- Heart – feeling positive and excited about a new future
- Hands – changing their behaviour in their daily work.

Early attempts to change business culture in Africa have been limited to Hearing and Head. Perhaps deploying a smattering of vision and values posters; holding some finger-wagging meetings with HR followed by obligatory worship of the new logo. In this scenario, as in my supermarket story, most employees never even see the culture change as an opportunity. Some walk right over it. Some take a peek but, uncomprehending, move on. Others turn sharply away to avoid getting involved.

But with a brand-led culture transformation programme – one that engages Heart and asks the Hands to try something new – we now have a better chance of success.

First published October 2016

Culture change is for life

I have a coffee pot that I once bought in Italy. Most Italian households have one, it's made by Bialetti. It's a simple affair: you put water in the bottom and coffee grounds in the middle. Then you put it on the hob for a few minutes and the boiling water passes through the coffee grounds to fill the top of the pot with hot coffee. There's a little safety valve in case you overfill it. And the only way for the brew to fail is allowing it to overcook. Producing delicious coffee is almost guaranteed.

Pouring it, however, is anything but. I guess that three times out of five I make a mess on the table, and not through my own carelessness. Knowing that pouring neatly is a challenge, I have developed strategies to optimise my performance.

I hold the pot at a certain angle (a combination of X- and Y-axis known only to me) and I judge it by eye. Like astronaut Jack Swigert flying the crippled Apollo 13 into a perfect re-entry, it's an entirely analogue procedure. Yet I crash and burn on a regular basis.

When I ask my friends why the pot should be so hit-and-miss, they say: 'Because it's Italian!' It looks great, it makes delicious coffee, but it's unreasonable to expect it to be perfect all the time. Like pouring coffee from my Bialetti, I have realised that building the the perfect organisational culture is an un-finishable task. That's something even the most controlling CEO needs to accept. In fact. the more controlling you are, the more likely you are to fail. That's because companies are comprised of quirky entities called human beings. Each one with his or her own hopes, fears and opinions. Each one feeling entitled to vary those dimensions almost daily. Try controlling that and you'll end up in the madhouse.

To maintain the correct perspective, I usually return to the etymology of the word 'company'. It comes from the Latin *companio*, one who daily eats bread with you. So, the idea of collaboration, the daily sharing of the hardships and staples of life with other people, is actually fundamental to a proper understanding of company culture.

It's time to wake up and smell the coffee. Culture must be collaborative. It can be improved, but never probably perfected.

First published May 2018

Here are five tips to align staff behaviour to brand promise:

▶ Brand Delivery Tip 1 – ask your staff

Anyone who works in Africa understands that we are still in the early days of building corporate cultures that work. We have built processes; and we have improved governance. We have introduced innovation and continuous self-improvement. We have learnt how to present ourselves to the Stock Exchange and in the media. But, go inside any business, and you'll find habitual behaviours that have evolved over time and become fixed. They aren't part of any conscious attempt to develop a culture that serves customers. And it's hard to make sense of them from the executive floor, as employees below always appear to be in Brownian Motion.

That's why I instinctively go back to brand when I am assisting companies to reshape their culture. Your brand, its values and what it promises the market are – in my view – the clearest expression of commercial intent. And much more motivating that the Mission Statement that we all thought was the bee's knees, two decades ago.

Mission Statements usually start well, but rapidly descend into confusion. Layer upon layer is added, by committee. The result is nonsense at worst, unintelligible at best. I mean unintelligible to the man in the lorry park or the lady in the canteen, looking for some direction in their own corner of the business.

By contrast, I prize a lovely true story about a cleaning lady at NASA. Asked what her job was, she told the TV interviewer that it was 'to put a man on the moon'. She was able to say this because someone had defined a clear Brand Promise for the organisation, and shared it with her in a motivational and relevant way.

So, does the leadership team have to define every behavioural expectation themselves? No, they don't. They have to do something a lot braver: ask their staff to help design the culture.

I'm currently deeply involved in changing a microfinance business; eight months into their cultural refit. It's moving on apace, but the senior management team is not distracted by its demands. Instead, they have the pleasure of reviewing progress every month, and learning what we are going to do next: me and their staff.

So far, we have addressed basic hygiene issues ranging from disgraceful staff washrooms to defining a Code of Conduct for every employee to sign. We've swept away the perpetual IT snagging list. We have reinvigorated a middle management team that now understands the value of talking to each other outside formal meetings.

We have appointed young employees Brand Ambasadors, and we have organised them into three groups. One, to improve Internal Communications. Another to contribute to better Marketing. And a third to focus on Talent Development. Not one of these young people has any experience in HR, Communications or Marketing.

Nor did a single one of these initiatives come from Management. They all came from a large hall session I call Design Café. Where staff, whose opinions has never been sought, are given the chance to contribute their ideas. Their enthusiasm is always infectious, and the programmes that result are sustainable because new content and new ideas surface all the time – and staff own the process.

So, to CEOs who are wondering where they will find the energy to drive culture change, I say one thing. Work smart: use the talent you already have, and you'll enjoy unexpected dividends.

First published January 2017

▶ Brand Delivery Tip 2 – master culture

One of great benefits of living in the connected age is that you never need to stop learning. And one of the insights you gain is that, if there is a challenge in the world, someone before you will have considered it.

In the profession of building a corporate culture. My own Chairman, Professor Nader Tavassoli **www.nadertavassoli.com** has made organisational behaviour change his life's work, and he's still a young man. Not for him a detached academic view of the value of an aligned culture. His work is illuminated with case studies from the world's most successful enterprises. And peppered with terms like ROI and PE Ratio, that evidence a truly results-based approach.

Before Prof. Nader, there were others who examined the organisation of human beings for the purpose of productive business growth. The giant amongst them was Professor Edgar Schein of the MIT Sloan School of Management in Cambridge, Massachusetts, USA. There he codified our understanding of many aspects of career development, group process consultation and organisational culture. Schein's model identifies three key elements in organisational cultures: Artefacts, Espoused Values and Assumptions

Artefacts include any tangible, overt or verbally identifiable elements in an organisation. Architecture; furniture; dress code; office jokes; company brands and their logos. Artefacts are the visible elements in a culture and should be recognisable and describable by outsiders.

Espoused Values are the organisation's stated values and rules of behaviour. They represent what the Executive desires. The extent to which they are delivered, or even understood, by staff varies very widely. In strong cultures, they guide how members represent the organisation to themselves and to others. Public statements of identity; company history; legends and heroes. Espoused values sometimes contain a projection for the future, of what the members hope the organisation will become.

Shared Assumptions are the deeply embedded, taken-for-granted employee behaviours that constitute the essence of culture. Typically, they are so well-integrated into the workplace dynamic that they are hard to recognise from within and completely invisible from outside. But in a broken culture, they are negative: loaded with issues that produce inertia.

As I move around the enterprises of the region, and touch their cultures, Schein's observations ring very true.

In addition, I find that many Africans have been conditioned by decades of autocratic leadership. So, the larger the company, the bigger the despotism and the more silent the workforce.

But here's some heartening news. Give African staff members the opportunity to share their ideas on how the Company can do things better, and the culture rapidly improves. Take some of their ideas and make them work, and all the natural enthusiasm and creativity of human beings comes to the surface. Not for nothing is one of Schein's best-selling culture books entitled: 'The gentle gentle art of asking instead of telling.'

First published June 2015

▶ Brand Delivery Tip 3 – employer brand

Advertising no longer has the universal impact it once did. We are now firmly in the age of the well-informed and critical customer. Aligning employee behaviour to deliver the Brand Promise is now a strategic imperative for business leaders. This, in turn, puts more responsibility on organisational leaders to define the role of employees in delivering better customer experiences.

And that process begins with Employer Branding. The ability to package the overall benefits of being an employee in such a way that staff members buy into a value greater the monthly pay cheque. US-based consultancy Employer Brand International **www.employerbrandinternational.com** has some illuminating content on the whole subject. They recommend, before drafting your Employer Branding statement, that you work through two important areas of debate.

First, create your Employee Platform. This requires you to achieve consensus on the following aspects of your intended employee experience:

- The nature of your recruitment and induction process
- The competitiveness of your pay and benefits
- Opportunities for career development
- Fair and open reward and recognition
- Internal communications approach
- Employee opinion research
- The quality of work environment.

Second, your Strategic Platform. Here you will need to consider and record consensus on the following:

- Your organisation's Vision, Mission and Values (I prefer to use Brand Promise and Brand Personality)

- Your corporate reputation and culture
- The nature of your leadership
- Your approach to people and performance management
- Your innovation strategy
- Your policy on Corporate Social Responsibility.

Following this framework will help to ensure that the promises made to customers by the company's corporate or consumer brands are matched by the promise delivered to employees by their employer brand.

Many HR people make the mistake of talking about Employer Branding as a talent acquisition or recruitment tool. But it has to be exploited further than that. It needs to become part of the employee experience throughout their tenure, and thus form the bedrock of the organisation's culture.

First published January 2016

▶ Brand Delivery Tip 4 – walk the talk

When I think of the millions that companies spend on shaping and communicating their brand offerings, I often wonder why they invest so little inculcating branded behaviours in staff.

Several years ago, a large UK bank briefed its Advertising Agency to develop a new brand positioning and an advertising campaign to support it. The Agency's Market Research team discovered that UK customers felt their banks were increasingly treating them like numbers, not people with their own individual needs. So, the Agency's strategy people worked with their creative team to develop a new slogan and campaign that proclaimed that their client was 'The Listening Bank'.

The idea that, at last, there was a bank with ears was well received by the public. The bank invested millions of pounds in the advertising campaign and thousands of new customers flocked into its branches. So far, so good.

A year later the bank dropped the campaign, and since then it has become a case study in failure. The bank had made two fundamental mistakes. Firstly, the leadership team had taken a short-term approach to their brand. Once they felt the market had heard the new claim, they reduced investment in media. When a big brand does this for more than a couple of months, consumers notice and begin to wonder why.

Secondly, and more importantly, the Listening Bank's staff didn't listen to customers any more than they had before. They simply did not deliver on the brand promise.

Prospective customers, looking for someone really interested in their needs, were met by bank staff who didn't have the time to listen. You see, they'd all been trained and incentivised to handle customers more quickly and efficiently – to reduce costs. So, this very clever initiative, which promised exactly what customers were looking for, alienated both prospective customers and the bank's own staff, who bore the brunt of customer disappointment.

This problem is more widespread than we'd like to think. Research recently published by Harvard Business Review reveals that in a typical organisation, 65% of the US workforce doesn't understand its overall business objectives and over 90% can't translate its promise and values into their own behaviour.

They may be able to recite their brand slogan, but they don't know what they have to do differently to deliver on the promise it makes.

First published September 2017

▶ Brand Delivery Tip 5 – create space

The world of work still needs an effective solution to the shaping of productive office spaces. Here in Africa, relatively few of us have the privilege of working in offices. Far more people work in small retail outlets, factories and out under the hot sun. For the modern office worker, anything seems better than the dark-panelled dens of the Public Sector, or the stark concrete and glass of academia. So, many of us feel happy when we see an open plan office. 'Here,' we say, 'is a modern company. I am going to enjoy working here.'

But sometimes we are disappointed. Personally, I have never liked open plan workspaces (even those with glassed-off offices for managers, and rooms for meetings). My first experience of them was in Europe, where huge spaces housing hundreds of people were eerily silent. I found that silence inhibiting: it was as if everybody was listening to every call I made. Consequently, I spent a lot of time making calls in meeting rooms.

To be honest, I have never found open plan offices in Africa to be silent. There is always a hubbub, and usually it's cheerful. But the problem here is that everything that happens becomes everybody's business. Work and personal matters combine in an endless buzz that increases tensions between colleagues. Then we have open plan environments where the bosses like to shout, creating apprehension and fear. These are truly counter-productive, as employees spend most of their time anticipating unwelcome attention.

Now, a new Harvard University study has conclusively shown the demerits of open plan. Two Fortune 500 companies planning to convert their premises to open plan offices agreed to let Harvard compare how employees interacted both before and after the change. Researchers Ethan Bernstein and Stephen Turban had 150 participating employees wear socio-metric badges for three weeks, both before and after the redesigns. These recorded wearers' movement, location, posture and, via infrared and sound sensors, their every conversation with colleagues. In parallel, the researchers quantified the text messages and emails sent.

The results have just been published. They show that, as the walls came down, so did employee interaction. Simultaneously, the number of emails and text messages shot up, which won't surprise anyone who has seen people who sit together emailing each other! Average face-to-face time decreased by 70 percent across the participating employees, while email use increased by up to 50 percent. 'Rather than prompting increasingly vibrant face-to-face collaboration, open architecture appeared to trigger a natural human response to socially withdraw from officemates', conclude the study's authors.

It's time we encouraged our architects to bend their minds to a different workspace solution.

First published January 2019

Let's meet a
Delivery Diva

Agnes Mwathi

Agnes Mwathi is the youngest of this book's featured experts, but already performs a senior role as the Group Talent and Human Resources Manager for the pan-African Fintech giant, DPO. She's a career Human Resources professional who has learnt her trade in the Kenyan Banking and Insurance sectors over the past fifteen years.

Most importantly she represents the new generation of talent-focused HR leaders who still number so few in Africa. But I fervently hope that her example will inspire a wholesale change in that profession.

Agnes gained a BSc. in International Business Administration at United States University, Africa. Then she took a Higher National Diploma in Human Resources Management and, more recently, has earned a Masters in Business Administration from Daystar University, Nairobi.

Agnes says: 'An organisation must look 'outside in' and build a culture that will deliver on the ever-changing needs of its customers. And to do this, the specific culture component and elements must be defined, communicated, measured and rewarded on an ongoing basis.'

www.thebrandinside.com
and **www.thebrandinsideafrica.com**

About the author

Chris Harrison

Chris is the Africa Partner of The Brand Inside, a global culture change consultancy which works inside major organisations to align staff behaviour to delivery of the brand promise. **www.thebrandinside.com** and **www.thebrandinsideafrica.com**

Chris launched The Brand Inside in Africa in 2015. Before this he was a Marketer and then an Advertising Executive for 20 years, starting as a Brand Manager with Bass plc and ending at Young & Rubicam Brands, where he was the Executive Chairman for Africa and the Indian Ocean, with responsibility for 22 markets.

With offices both in Nairobi and Johannesburg, The Brand Inside already has clients in five countries and is changing internal cultures in a range of economic sectors including Agriculture, Commodities, Conservation, Education, Fashion, Fintech, Food, Healthcare, ICT, Insurance, Logistics, Manufacturing, Microfinance, NGO, Security and Tourism. For nearly a decade, Chris has written weekly columns on branding and culture in Africa's national newspapers. His observations may be found on his personal blog site **www.companycultures.guru**

Chris is a member of the Superbrands panel for East Africa. He served as a Council Member of the Marketing Society of Kenya and was Secretary and then Chairman of the Advertising Practitioners Association of Kenya for many years. He was Chairman of the charity British Legion Kenya, and of The Kenya Fly Fishers' Club. He also served as an Independent Director at Mayfair Insurance.

In 2018, he co-founded Amalgam Leadership, East Africa's only CEO development programme delivering applicable business learning, written and delivered by experienced CEOs for newly-appointed business leaders **www.amalgamleadership.com**

Chris holds an MA (Honours) degree in Medieval History with Archaeology from the University of St. Andrews, and is a graduate both of the McCann Global Leadership Programme at Columbia University and of several Brand Management programmes from the Chartered Institute of Marketing. He is also a member of the UK's Institute of Directors.

A Briton, he has worked in Africa for 25 years.

www.ingramcontent.com/pod-product-compliance
Lightning Source LLC
Chambersburg PA
CBHW070229180526
45158CB00001BA/275